Your Life or Your Debt

Andrew J. Ruiz, III

Book cover design by Ebooklaunch.com

ISBN 978-0-578-71619-0

For more information email AJR@eatel.net

FIRST EDITION

Contents

Acknowledgements

Having the opportunity to write this book and unfold these real life stories so that others in similar circumstances could benefit was an incredible personal journey for me. As with any large undertaking, I had many supporters who helped make this possible.

First and foremost, I thank God for giving me His strength, wisdom, and guidance to accomplish this project, for without Him I can do nothing. I thank Him for giving me a heart to listen and gain wisdom and the opportunity to share this path for many to get out of debt.

This grand task would not have been possible without the help and support of my wife, Shannon, who did her best to keep me free from distractions while writing and was always willing to listen to my many random thoughts, ideas and struggles along the way.

To my beautiful children, Rachel, Johnny and Luke who have grown me in ways I didn't know I needed as I navigated the joys and challenges of fatherhood. It pleases me to see each of them grow into kind and responsible young adults who will hopefully use this book as a guide in their own lives.

To my father Andrew Ruiz Jr. who has given me the foundation of knowledge and wisdom and has guided me not only through life and business but also throughout this book.

In memory of my late mother, Barbara Labbe' Ruiz who provided the fertile soil in our home through her loving and nurturing character, in which we were able to flourish and grow into our God given purposes.

To my brother Charles Ruiz and partner in business, who took a leap of faith with me over twenty-five years ago into the unknowns of becoming business owners and whose support to me over the years has helped this book become reality.

And finally, my friend Leon Contavasprie who along the way encouraged and guided me throughout this book.

INTRODUCTION

Having managed a Collection Agency for over three decades, I have had the opportunity to speak with thousands of ordinary folks whose lives have become filled with debt. I have witnessed firsthand the destruction that debt can cause and the impact it has on families all across America; from upper class to lower class; from older generations, who have simply failed to plan to younger generations, who have put more effort into selecting cell phone ring tones and alerts than they have put into organizing their own finances; men and women of all ages, in the same boat and faced with the same dismal financial predicament. Debt does not distinguish as it destroys and rips apart the hopes and dreams of individuals and families.

Gone is the hope, promise and dreams that once filled the lives of these families and individuals. The accumulated debt has become such a dominate player in their lives that they cannot think or see past it. So, they stopped dreaming and have lost hope for a brighter future.

For these families, every month was a battle to try and make the dollars work, as if trying to fit a square peg in a round hole. Regardless of how hard they worked to crunch the numbers, they continuously fall short, month after month while digging a deeper hole. With the math they were using, the numbers were never going to fit or make sense, unless drastic, across the board changes were made in their lives.

The financial decisions that these individuals and families have made are having lasting effects, and these effects will be felt for many years to come. Everyone in the family suffers equally and pays the price for the lack of financial planning, supervision, and reckless spending. No one in the family is immune from the consequences that come with the accumulation of debt. The entire family feels the effects of debt, in one way or another once it is dragged into the household.

I was curious and wanted to know what had happened in the lives of these folks. What factors played a role in the financial decisions that were made to have them end up in such dire financial distress? So, I asked the tough questions so that young families and others just starting out might avoid the roads these individuals and families traveled.

I interviewed people willing to share their story, ordinary people from all walks of life, some with college degrees and some who did not even finish high school. You will read their stories scattered throughout this book. I changed their names to protect their privacy.

All of these people you will read about have uniquely different stories of how they arrived at this desperate point in their lives, where the debt they have accumulated is now the dominate player which now rules over their lives.
They come from different backgrounds and income levels. Some of these people earn six-digit incomes, some earn five-digit incomes and some even attempt to survive on a four-digit annual salary. Regardless of their income or social status, none of them had the ability to meet their monthly obligations.

They all share the guilt of living large and way beyond what their paychecks could back up. Regardless of their income, they are all guilty of overspending.

They now find themselves walking a financial tight rope with no safety net and absolutely no room for error. With the finances extremely tight in their lives, they cannot afford for anything to break or go wrong in any given month because of their decisions to buy now and pay whenever. These families are all too familiar with the emotions that come with being in debt. Stress, despair, loneliness, powerlessness, hopelessness, and shame all describe the effects of debt. Because of the constant financial stress these individuals endure day and night, their physical and mental state is being pushed to the limit, to say the least. Their spouses and children must walk on eggshells around the house for fear of igniting a spark which could set off an angry tirade, caused by the overwhelming pressure of debt.

Some have lost the dignity and financial freedom they once enjoyed, due to the decision to accumulate stuff and more stuff which could not be afforded. Now these unpaid for toys and gadgets clutter their homes and serve as a constant reminder of what they traded their freedom for. They have lost the ability to do what they want, when they want, on their own terms. Now, they must abide and take orders from creditors and are told how much and when to pay.

They all wonder what went wrong in their lives that have allowed them to arrive at such a lonely desperate point. Most have trouble remembering what life was like before they began swimming in debt. Some must travel way back to their teenage years to arrive at peaceful memories of not being in debt.

None of these people had planned for their lives to turn out like this. It is as if, the debt just appeared out of nowhere and swallowed them without any warning. By wandering around life with no spending plan, it was just a matter of time before life dealt them a cruel hand that they were unprepared to handle.

Most of their stories have two common denominators, reckless spending, and no savings in place to handle even the smallest emergencies that arose. Their rainy-day fund consisted only of hoping for no rain! None of these folks had planned on anything bad or unexpected happening in their lives. Words like *proactive* and *preemptive* were not part of their vocabulary, but now words like *reactive* and *responsive* are very much a part of it.

Nothing was going to stand in their way of living to purchase. They felt financially invincible and feared absolutely nothing. It did not matter if there was instability at the workplace or the condition of the economy. None of that was factored in, because they were too focused on getting the newest gadget, upgrading to the newest cell phone or getting the latest and greatest television to realize the warning signs and the dangers that lie ahead with the purchasing of these items on credit.

None of these people had a solid plan for their paychecks once it arrived. Their money was already gone before they even had a chance to touch the paycheck. These people were caught up in the merry-go-round of spending and had trouble getting off.

Nobody was paying attention to the money. It took being placed in collections for them to realize just how bad their financial situations had deteriorated. For some, it was a wakeup call and a turning point in their lives. For others, it was no big deal, just another collection agency to deal with.

Why did these people speak with us? Because we treated them with respect! Respect that anyone in this situation would have wanted to be treated with! We asked them if they would be willing to share their set of circumstances which lead them into debt. Most of these people had never shared their story and were very anxious and curious to tell their side of the story, a way to vindicate themselves of the guilt of living beyond their means. Some were baffled as to why anyone would care or want to know what caused them to go into debt. It was as if they expected that everyone would always have some form of debt issues to deal with in life.

Some had also tried to validate their reasons for going into debt, as if to shift the blame on the circumstances that life threw at them. Circumstances they feel could not have been avoided. The bottom line was plain and simple. They did not have any goals or a solid game plan for their money. The money that came in each month left the same month; it was that simple.

These people are now all searching in one way or another for a way to escape the debt traps they are now caught in; an avenue to take them back home, to a time when things were simple and not so complicated. Some were optimistic that they could turn their financial situations around and free themselves of the debt. Some were not so optimistic and just willing to accept the fact that this is how life will always be.

Without a plan in place to supervise and direct the money, the money was able to do what it wanted to do with absolutely no curfews, no rules and no restrictions, it was able to roam freely and do as it pleased. And it did!

By not establishing a plan or a goal in life, there is no direction, no guidance, no goals to aim for or to keep you motivated and on course to finish strong. These people did not purposely plan to fail financially. They simply underestimated life and did not have a solid plan for their money and were not prepared to combat the financial difficulties that life hurled at them, month after month. Without any financial goals to shoot for, there was nothing to hold them accountable in their day to day spending.

1. Larry's Story

In the game of basketball, position is everything if you want to win. It is crucial for a player to establish position on his opponent, to get a decent shot off or to block the opponent from driving to the basket.

Establishing financial position in life is also important if you want to win with money. By having a solid financial position, you will have the freedom and flexibility to be able to make choices that will enhance your life, rather than making choices out of financial necessity. By having financial freedom and flexibility, your odds at succeeding and having a much more fulfilling life is greater.
Being in position to take a shot when life calls is much more important than being in position to take a shot in basketball. For Larry, it was more about being out of position when opportunity came knocking on his door.

Larry had worked part-time for a local supermarket chain during his high school years. The supermarkets were family-owned, consisting of three stores, all within a ten-mile radius of each other. Construction plans for an additional store were also in the works. The small chain had a great reputation for management, cleanliness, quality customer service and competitive pricing. Store sales were reflective of their customer loyalty, as they continued to rise every year.

Larry was well liked and respected by the store owner and was treated more like a son than an employee. Larry was offered a full-time position with the store at the location of his choice upon graduating from high school. Larry was grateful for the job offer, but he and his father had much bigger plans after graduation, namely going to college and pursuing an engineering degree.

Larry seemed to have a knack for the supermarket business and could run every phase of the store. He quickly developed a reputation for being a dependable, hard worker. Larry really enjoyed his job and found it rewarding. He especially enjoyed helping and getting to know the customers. Larry looked forward to going to work with great enthusiasm and it was reflected in his effort and attitude. He was practically on a first name basis with hundreds of customers that he had met through the years.

Upon graduating from high school, Larry immediately enrolled in college to pursue his goal of getting an engineering degree.
Larry had attended an out of town college, so when he would come home on the weekends, he would manage to get in a few hours of work at the store. The owner was very accommodating to Larry's schedule and felt lucky to get him whenever he could. The commute from Larry's college to the store was about a two-hour drive.

Larry was majoring in Civil Engineering and planned to follow in his father's footsteps. Larry's father had been with the same engineering firm for the past 25 years and was hoping to get his son a job with the prestigious firm after graduation.

All throughout Larry's college career, he managed to continue to work at the store almost every weekend, except when a major event was taking place on campus. Larry's college days just seemed to fly by as it was a special time in his life.

By the time, he entered his fifth year of college; Larry had amassed nearly $11,000 in credit card debt along with his entire college tuition in the form of student loans. He was aware of the debt that had been accumulating but figured that with a future full-time salary clearing the balance would be easy.

It was not until Larry's last year in college that he really started to do the math and worry about the debt that had racked up over the years. Along with the debt on his mind, he also started to question his chosen career field. He wondered if being an engineer was what he really wanted to do with his life or was he just fulfilling his father's wishes. Larry had a lot of pressure on him and some tough decisions had to be made in his final year of college.

Larry's mind was filled with anxiety and uncertainty as he struggled with his future and the debt that he had accumulated. Larry knew that one day he would have to face the mounting student loan debt head on but refused to let it slow him down during what was supposed to be the best years of his life. Many of Larry's friends also had their tuition financed though student loans and they did not seem to be sweating it. They all were of the same mind set once they landed that dream job, the student loan debt would not be a problem.
It took Larry just under five years to complete his college career and earn his degree. During this five-year stretch, he managed to rack up almost $68,000 in federal student loans along with the $11,000 in credit card debt.

Larry's college education was financed 100% through student loans. His part time job at the supermarket, along with credit cards, paid for his housing, clothes, gas, food, and whatever other expenses would come up. What he did not realize is that student loans become due shortly after graduating or dropping out of college, regardless if you receive a degree, or have a job.

As expected, Larry was offered a job with his father's company. His excitement was tempered only by the desperate need of income with his student loans coming due soon. Besides the student loan payments, Larry also had to contend with his credit card debt. Suddenly, it seemed Larry's life had shifted into high gear. Gone, were the carefree days of college. Larry could no longer hold on to the laid-back student life he had known for five years; he now had a full-time job along with the fancy title of "young professional." Trailing not far behind the new title was his debt.

After two years with the engineering firm, it became evident to Larry that this was not his calling in life. He was certain that he made a mistake going into the engineering field. He was not happy or fulfilled with the work he was doing. Larry dreaded waking up in the mornings and going to work. He was sick and tired of faking a career that was not meant to be. No longer could he continue living this life. This was not the kind of life Larry had envisioned for himself and he was not going to pretend any longer. To a degree, he resented his father because he felt that if it hadn't been for his father's persistence, he would have probably never gone to college to pursue the engineering degree and would have gone to work for the supermarket.

He often wondered what his life would have been like if he had accepted the supermarket job, right out of high school. He certainly would not have the student loan debt to contend with every month. Larry was reminded of this every month as his loan payment would come due. Although the pay at the supermarket was not close to what he was making now, he enjoyed working in the store and really missed it. He truly wished he had taken the supermarket road instead of the path that he was currently on. He might not be making as much money but at least he would have been happier and doing what he enjoyed.

Larry felt like a prisoner in his apartment. The debt that Larry carried were the handcuffs that kept him from living his life on his own terms rather than the banks terms. By carrying such high levels of debt, Larry was unable to financially stretch and live how he wanted to live. The debt was slowly consuming and taking over control of his young life. He felt helpless and lonely, as if there was no clear path out of this nightmare.

Larry wondered; how would people view him? Would he be viewed as a failure if he were not working in the field in which he had studied? How many degreed engineers do you see working in a supermarket? How many fools go way into debt to become an engineer only to not become one?

Larry did the math and figured that if he had gone to work at the supermarket, he would have earned roughly $40,000 a year, which would have earned him close to $200,000 in the five-year period he attended college. Instead of earning $200,000, he had amassed $68,000 in student loans and $11,000 in credit card debt.

Larry also came to the realization that he could not afford to leave his employer. All this talk about what he should or should not have done was meaningless. Larry knew the facts, he owed $68,000 that needed to be paid back.

He realized that he was literally stuck in his job whether he liked it or not. All it would take would be one missing

monthly check and he would be in a financial tailspin. Things were tight financially, to say the least. Even though he never missed a paycheck, bills still fell delinquent.
To make matters worse, Larry was juggling additional debt totaling $38,000, including a new car that he purchased a year into his new job along with $3,000 in new purchases that were put on credit since graduating college. This new debt, along with the $11,000 which was racked up in college, now brought his total debt including the student loan to a whopping $117,000

Larry was not in a financial position to entertain the thought of leaving his company. He began to question his decision to pile up student loan debt, along with credit card debt. This only compounded the problem of not being fulfilled in his chosen field. He now has two serious issues to deal with at the same time; the fact that he is not happy with work and his heavy debt load.

Larry went so far as to entertain the thought of filing bankruptcy on the student loan debt, until he found out after consulting with a bankruptcy attorney, that you cannot bankrupt federal student loans. The student loan debt was like an endangered species; it was protected and could not be wiped out. Larry also learned that along with student loan debt, alimony, child support and money owed to the IRS cannot be included in bankruptcy filings.
Larry was desperate and to the point, where he was looking for any way out of his financial mess and was willing to consider any method that could get him out. He was simply miserable.

The decisions that Larry made in the past seven years have come back to haunt him and are now dictating his every move. He is now "out of position" in life and unable to call his own shots. Because of his financial situation, he does not have the leverage to entertain any lesser paying job opportunities that might become available, including a position at the supermarket.

Believe it or not, Larry's situation is only temporary. If he can control his lifestyle and spending so that his focus can be on paying off this debt, he can regain control of his life and point it in a new direction. His lifestyle played a big part in getting him in this financial mess and a new lifestyle can play a big part in getting him out.

2. LARRY'S PATH TO FREEDOM

Larry refused to be held captive by his debt or his job at the engineering firm. After some serious sole searching, he realized that he would rather take a pay cut than be stuck in a field that he neither enjoyed nor found rewarding. His first mission was to declare war on his debt. Coming up with a plan to eliminate the debt would be Larry's first step to gaining his freedom back. Life was too short, and Larry was not about to be questioning his decisions thirty years down the road. He wanted to lead a fulfilling life and it was not going to happen at his current job.

His first plan of attack was to see exactly what he was up against.
He cleared his kitchen table and laid out all his bills to get an accurate view. He knew who the major players were but wanted to get the exact figure of his indebtedness.
He had decided that he was going to come up with an aggressive plan to rid his debt once and for all. If getting rid of the debt meant working eighty-plus hours a week, then so be it. The one thing Larry was not afraid of was hard work.

The first phase in Larry's attack was to increase his income so that he could speed up his plan to eliminate the debt. His first thought was to see if the supermarket would hire him as a part-time employee. Larry figured he could work evenings and weekends. The money he earned from the supermarket job would be dedicated exclusively to wiping out his debt.

Larry was pumped and excited because of the renewed hope and freedom that his plan offered. He could hardly sleep that night, as he was eager and ready to put his plan into motion. He was prepared to swallow his pride by working at the supermarket to supplement his income.

The next day, Larry had planned visiting Mr. Hines, the supermarket owner. Larry had kept in touch over the years and felt confident that he would hire him on a part-time basis.
Mr. Hines was excited to see Larry walk through the doors. The two spoke for hours, catching up on what had been happening in their lives. Larry had confessed to Mr. Hines that he made a mistake going into the field of engineering and accumulating a mountain of debt which was keeping him tied to the engineering firm.

Once Larry had revealed his wish to return to the store on a part-time basis, Mr. Hines was ecstatic. Mr. Hines was also willing to accommodate Larry and give him any schedule that he wanted. Mr. Hines went even further by paying Larry closer to what his full-time employees were earning.

Larry was anxious to get going and started working immediately. He was a valuable employee to the store because he could wear many different hats and he knew the day-to-day operations like the back of his hand. For Larry, returning to the supermarket was like getting back on a bicycle that had not been ridden in years. Larry hit the ground running, and it did not take long for it to all come back to him. Some outdated methods of the grocery operation that Larry was used to were replaced with newer, more efficient technology. Even with the new technology, it did not take long for Larry to catch on.
Larry had figured he better notify his colleagues at the engineering firm that he was working part-time at the

supermarket. He did not want to shock his co-workers at the firm if they did run across him at the store, since it was only about three miles from the firm. Larry personally did not care what anybody thought about him working at the store, he was only interested in wiping out the debt.

Larry had the extra income phase of his plan now in motion. He then focused on shaving his lifestyle and shedding debt. Larry started thinking outside the box and getting radical on ways to eliminate the debt from his life. He first examined his two largest expenses that could be cut - his apartment rent and his vehicle. Larry knew that his parents would not mind if he moved back home temporarily to eliminate the nearly $900 monthly rent. He did the calculations in his head and realized that he could save $10,800 a year on rent by moving in with his parents.
Next, he listed his car for sale. Once the sale was final, he was prepared to pay cash to purchase a used car. He figured that after the sale, he would probably still owe around $1,500 to the bank since more was owed on the car than what it would sell for. This was confirmed after looking at the current values on his make and model through Kelly's blue book. By getting rid of the car, Larry could save an additional $425 monthly.

With three years remaining on the car loan, he could save $15,300, minus the amount that was still owed on the car after the sale. The apartment rent and the car represented roughly $26,000 worth of bondage which was now gone from Larry's life. The money that previously went toward the car and the apartment would now be re-directed toward the outstanding debt. Larry hated to see the car go but his financial freedom was much more valuable than a new car. With the car out of his life, he could feel the shackles start to loosen a little, which really got Larry even more fired up. Larry's plan was on fire and that fired him up!

Larry always showed up for work at the supermarket with a smile on his face and an eagerness to work, even after already working an eight-hour day at the engineering firm. Larry looked forward to the weekends, because he could focus on one job and only eight hours days, instead of the 13-14 hours days he carried during the week. Some weekends he had off altogether and would use that precious time for rest. Mr. Hines honestly did not know how long Larry would be able to keep up this ferocious work pace. Larry kept defying the odds, week after week, by showing up to work always with a smile. This only reinforced how Mr. Hines had felt about Larry's work habits, dedication, and his determination to follow through on the goals that he set.

Larry's lifestyle had been reduced strictly to work. As time went on, his debt started to diminish. Seeing this, Larry became even more focused on wiping out the remaining debt. The more debt he wiped out, the more excited he got. Wiping out the debt was an incredible high that kept Larry focused and determined. He consistently worked close to 40 hours a week at the supermarket, along with 40 hours going to the engineering firm each week.

In less than two years of strict dedication and focus, Larry had reduced his debt to zero and was finally able to taste and fully appreciate complete financial freedom. Larry was completely debt free and had accomplished the goal that he had set. To know that he was truly liberated was an incredible feeling of accomplishment, one that he had trouble putting into words without becoming emotional. This was an incredible life journey that Larry had embarked on and one that he would continue to build on for the rest of his life.

One evening, as Larry was clocking out from the store, Mr. Hines had asked him to stop by his office for a brief meeting. The two discussed Larry's future goals and plans now that the debt was officially eliminated. Mr. Hines explained to Larry that he had planned on retiring soon and would need someone to oversee the day-to-day operations of all the stores. Larry listened intently as Mr. Hines offered him a full-time job as district manager. This was a new position that Mr. Hines was creating since he had personally overseen all the stores in the past. Larry was thrilled with the offer and accepted the job without hesitation as he hugged Mr. Hines. Larry was offered a base salary of $60,000 along with a quarterly bonus, which was tied to each store's performance.

The lessons that Larry had learned in the past couple of years would truly benefit him in his new management role. Larry took charge of his bleak financial situation and was determined to eventually gain back control of his life. Larry could have easily settled into his job as an engineer, but he was not content in that role and was determined to do whatever it took to create new options.

Larry took charge of his new position as district manager with great enthusiasm. The excitement and energy that he brought to the job rubbed off on everyone in the store.
In his second full year as district manager, sales were at an all-time high and employee turnover was at an all-time low which exceeded everyone's expectations, including Mr. Hines. Larry had earned more in that second year on the job than he had ever earned in his life. Most importantly, he was in a job that he enjoyed, a job that he had no problem getting out of bed each morning to report to.

3. Debt and the Quality of Living

Weather certainly plays a big role in our day-to-day planning. It directly influences what we can do and how we dress. The weather also sets the tone for our moods. If it is a gloomy day, our mood is often one of gloom. If it is sunny, our mood is more of a cheerful one. So, to say that weather has a huge impact on our lives is an accurate statement. Debt is also something that can influence the way we act and feel. It also plays a big part in our quality of living.

Of all the problems that could potentially plague families, debt is one problem that the whole family can actively take part in helping to tame and eliminate.

For families that are burdened by debt, their quality of living is directly influenced by the debt they carry. Debt and the quality of living flow in the opposite directions and work against each other. Therefore, the greater the debt, the lower the quality of living and the lower the debt, the higher the quality of living!

Quality of life paired with debt are just not a good fit and can be compared to oil and water or cats and dogs. They do not fit comfortably and do not go good together, ever! The level of debt plays a big part in the attitudes and tensions that exist in families. If parents are heavily burdened by debt, their attitudes and moods will flow down and negatively affect the children.

It is safe to say that debt is not an individual affair, it is a family affair. The effects of debt do not discriminate and are equally distributed to the whole family. Having debt is like having the flu. Regardless how it finds its way into the home, over time the whole family is certain to feel the effects in one way or another. The key to eliminating debt is to know where to look! Once you have successfully located the root of the problem (what is causing the pain) you can start to devise a plan to attack it. When you are burdened by debt, pinpointing the root of the problem is not difficult. Simply, look around and follow the money trail and you will locate the problem. A good place to start looking is in the house. Catalog everything that is not paid for and you will find the root of the problem.

If your family is plagued by debt, you are not alone. Many families are facing this problem and are working to ease the pain in their life that debt has caused. Of all the problems that have the potential to affect families, debt is a problem that when dissected, is not extremely difficult to understand. There is usually a clear-cut answer to the question, "What happened to our finances? How did we manage to get to this desperate point?" The answer in most cases will always be, "We spent more than we made!"

The magic formula to conquering and staying out of debt is outgo<intake=financial stability Very simply, your outgo (expenses) must always be less than your intake (income). If you have solved this equation, Congratulations! You have figured out the key to beating debt. If you can successfully apply this formula to your household finances, you can begin to get out of debt and stay out of debt.
It is not a complicated equation. Families must spend less than what they make. This formula has a proven track record that works. By addressing the debt problem, the quality of life problem automatically starts to improve on its own. Of all the people I interviewed for this book that were in debt, roughly 95% said that the biggest obstacle affecting their quality of living was debt.

If your quality of life is suffering, there is a great chance you are overloaded with debt. The good news is that debt is a fixable problem. Debt is something that you can sink your teeth into and tackle immediately by making cuts and sacrificing lifestyles. This will bring instant relief and start you on the road to living a fulfilled life.

4. Hiding Debt in a Marriage (Ralph and Jill's Story)

Marriages take a lot of work and sacrifice to keep them healthy and going strong. They are challenging and rewarding and worth fighting for. Marriages have a tough time surviving on their own, without distractions playing into the mix. By introducing distractions, focus is shifted away from the marriage to whatever outside influence has been introduced. There are many outside influences which can creep into a marriage with debt and finances being one of the top infiltrators.

When debt creeps into a marriage, a new element is introduced, and a new player must be accommodated. This new player (debt) brings incredible stress into marriages, especially young ones and requires a ton of time and energy. Attention is diverted from the marriage and shifts towards the debt which has taken center stage and becomes the focus and point of contention. Debt has a way of festering in a marriage over time and can slowly begin to erode the foundation and principles on which the marriage was built, if the proper urgency is not applied to address the debt.

Debt can be introduced into a marriage in two ways. It is either accumulated before the marriage and enters at the altar or it is accumulated after the wedding. However, the debt penetrates the marriage, it must be confronted and dealt with. Without a strong foundation to battle the debt, it is just a matter of time before the debt starts to take a toll on marriages.

In Ralph and Jill's case, bringing debt into the marriage didn't seem to bother either one. Both had accumulated a sizeable amount of debt before entering the marriage.
Shortly after getting engaged, the topic of debt was discussed, but without a lot of emphasis or urgency placed on getting rid of it. They agreed that each would take care of their own incurred debt, out of their own separate checking accounts. Both had good careers with good income, so the debt wasn't top priority.

Jill had approximately $25,000 of debt, most of which was student loans and Ralph was contributing about $15,000, mostly comprised of credit card debt. Neither Ralph nor Jill had any savings or an emergency fund to fall back on in the event of an unforeseen emergency.

In their first year of marriage, the couple wasted no time moving into a new home and filling it with fancy new furniture. Jill wanted nothing to do with the furniture that Ralph had shared with his first wife, so it was agreed upon that they would start fresh with brand new, unpaid for furniture for their new home. The couple spared no expense in loading up their dream house with nothing but the finest furniture and appliances.

With a complete newly furnished home, the couple loved to entertain by having friends and family over to show off their new digs while Ralph dazzled them with his gourmet cooking skills. They were especially proud of their outside bar along with a gas top stove where most of the entertaining took place. Ralph was somewhat of a chef and loved to prepare and test new dishes for his friends and family.
Jill and Ralph also loved to travel to foreign countries to experience new cultures and new cuisine. They figured they would get their overseas trips out of the way before

starting a family. All their travel was financed courtesy of credit cards. The first two years of the marriage was filled with trips to four different continents.

One evening as Jill was sifting through the mail, she noticed something from the United States Postal Service addressed to Ralph. It was a notice that a $60 annual fee was due for the rental of a post office box. Jill found this to be very odd and figured there must be some mistake because their mail is delivered directly to their door not a post office box. Since Ralph was out of town for a week on business, Jill didn't bother him about it or pay much attention to it and figured it might have been an old Post Office box that Ralph once shared with his first wife.

A couple of days had gone by and Jill found herself still very curious over the letter. She found it very odd that her husband would have a P.O. Box and not tell her about it. Jill could not get that letter out of her mind and didn't mention anything to Ralph as they spoke on the phone each night.

Later one night, as Jill was going through her husband's drawer, she discovered a key that looked like it might be a fit for a postal box. On the key it read "property of the U.S. Postal Service, do not duplicate." Jill didn't know what to think as these thoughts raced through her mind. She kept asking herself, "why? Why would my husband have a post office box and not tell me about it?" Their marriage was going on its third year; surely, he had ample time to mention this to her. Jill's thoughts got the best of her as her mind raced in all directions.

The next morning, Jill had decided to stop on her way into work at the local post office to investigate. Having no idea what box number it matched, she told the clerk that she forgot what box number her husband had told her to check. After giving the clerk her husband's name, Jill proceeded nervously as she walked to the box number that matched the key.

As Jill opened the box, she was astounded to find mail, almost an inch thick. Mostly credit card bills and demand letters from collection agencies. She soon realized that her husband had been hiding debt from her. Jill now wondered what else, might her husband be hiding.

When Ralph returned home from his trip, he was greeted by a stack of mail on the kitchen counter and a very hurt wife. After realizing that the mail had a P.O. Box address on it, he soon realized what had transpired while he was away. He put two and two together and figured, he had some explaining to do.

That night, after a tearful confession, Ralph came clean and laid everything on the table. He confessed to Jill that his debt was much greater than the amount he had originally stated before they were married. Ralph figured that if Jill knew the true figure of his debt, she would not have agreed to continue with the relationship. Ralph figured that by hiding the debt, he might be able to pay it off and Jill would never know the true amount owed. Unfortunately, their lifestyle prevented him from making any substantial progress on his plan to pay down the debt. The total amount of Ralph's "newly exposed" debt was $74,300.

With the debt now out in the open, in full view, both were ready to move forward after a humble heart-felt apology and a forgiving and understanding wife.

Ralph felt as if a ton of bricks had been lifted off him with the confession of his debt. He was thankful for the series of

events unfolding the way it did. At least now with the debt out in the open, Ralph was liberated by the truth.
Ralph loved his wife deeply and didn't intend to hurt her by not telling her about the debt, but with each passing day it got harder and harder to bring it up.

He feared that if he told her the truth, she would not trust him anymore and their relationship would start to decline. The pressure of not being honest with his wife was beginning to take a toll on Ralph. The stress, guilt and lies caused Ralph to lose sleep and not feel good about himself as a husband and leader.

Ralph knew all of this could have been avoided by being honest with his wife and more responsible with his spending in the first place.
Ralph was finally looking forward to a good night's sleep, now that all the lies were exposed and had nowhere to hide. With the stress of his wife not knowing about the hidden debt now behind him, it was time to move forward and implement a plan of action to put the debt to rest permanently. With the latest revelation of Ralph's newfound debt, the couple realized the scope of how serious their debt problem had become. Financially, the couple went from living on the edge to a fallen off the cliff situation. Now it was time to start the climb back up the cliff.

For the first time in their short marriage, Ralph and Jill were forced to work as a team and face their debt head on. Their first order of business was to have one checking account. Gone were the individual checking accounts along with the phrase his or hers. They now referred to themselves as one and they referred to the debt as theirs.

Immediately, they began to target ways to cut and save in order to pay more towards the debt. They began pursuing knowledge on how to avoid debt and dig out from under the pile they had already accumulated. Together they began to pray and read what the bible had to say about money and debt.

From that point forward, they worked hard on coming up with a budget and cutting expenses. Both were determined that debt was not going to stand between them in their marriage or rule their lives. They both made big sacrifices and sold items in order to get their repayment plan off to a strong start. The $60 bill that was going to be paid to the post office is now being redirected and applied to the couple's debt.

As Ralph and Jill sacrificed and stripped their lives of possessions, they learned how to avoid future debt and began to grow together as a couple.
The debt that once threatened to rip their young marriage apart had miraculously managed to bring them closer than ever. Their foreign trips have now been put on hold, along with their lifestyle, while they worked to clear up the debt.

Debt is hardly ever discussed or is even an issue when things are going well in a household. Most families that have debt realize that a plan must be established to address and tackle it, but that plan is usually pushed aside until after Christmas.
Once the New Year is ushered in, resolutions are made to cut back and pay more towards the debt but usually that doesn't last due to the lack of urgency and focus since things are going just fine the way they are.

Very seldom is a debt repayment plan executed when the going is good. It usually takes a catastrophic event to shake up a family.

The minute a salary disappears due to a job loss, it's a different story. It's as if a debt bomb went off in the living room and everyone is wondering what happened. All eyes are now intently focused on the debt that needs to be fed, as if it is a hungry elephant in the house that has just awoken. Now that it's awake it has everyone's full attention. Panic suddenly starts to set in, as if the debt is rearing its ugly head for the first time. During the good times, the debt is simply swept under the rug and ignored. Once the rug is picked up, it's a different ball game with the debt now exposed and in full view for everyone to see. Don't wait for a financial catastrophe to happen in your household before you get your finances in order.

With Finances being one of the top reasons couples divorce it is crucial that marriages address debt and try to avoid it at all costs. With all the risks and dangers that come with debt, it's just not worth jeopardizing your marriage in order to satisfy a need or fill a void by spending money you don't have.

The national divorce rate is around 50%. Imagine how low the rate would drop by eliminating debt problems from marriages altogether? How would divorce Attorney's make a living if marriages were held together?

You can't build and nurture a relationship if you are constantly addressing and fighting over debt issues. Your attention will be spilt and not focused on your spouse. Debt is like a disease, it will fester and eventually destroy the whole family, if forgotten about and left untreated. Credit gives couples freedom and enables them to purchase anything under the sun but with credit comes debt and debt doesn't guarantee the survival of a marriage.

5. Living Large

More and more individuals and families are sliding deeper and deeper into debt, because of living too large and spending too freely. By having the security of an income, families and individuals feel financially invincible. They throw caution out the window, while they live for the day and fear nothing. They put all of their trust in their jobs and hope that the economy will not slow down.
Instead of these individuals and families being filled with hope and dreams, their lives are often only filled with debt and an uncertain future which always comes with over spending. With debt being the dominant player in their lives, it dictates how they live out their years and what they now spend their money on. Families are slowly being torn apart and the problem stems from living beyond their means and not knowing when to say "enough" while in front of the cash register.

In most cases, the debt incurred was self-inflicted, by careless and frivolous spending and no emergency buffer fund to tackle unexpected expenses. In other case's the debt was incurred by some type of addiction. Addiction's in the form of alcoholism, gambling, drugs and even shopping to some degree.

When closely examined, it is easy to see why families are in the predicament they are in. They are living too large! They are living in houses they cannot afford. They are driving cars they cannot afford and have their children in schools they cannot afford. Their homes are filled with electronics that are not paid for, and they eat in restaurants when they should be eating at their kitchen tables. The way these families are living, they are inches away from stepping on financial land minds, ready to explode at any second and blow their whole world up.

On a pack of cigarettes, we see mandatory warnings from the surgeon general about the dangers of smoking. Warning labels should also come on items purchased on credit, stating "if you buy this item on credit, you could go into debt; the risks outweigh the reward. So, please put some thought into this purchase before you decided to charge this item."

Families that make $40k a year often live and buy like they make $75k a year, while many families that are unemployed are still living like they are employed. They are living for the moment and not giving any thought to their future or their family's future.

Most feel invincible, as if nothing can rock their world simply because they are currently employed, when in fact, it does not take much at all to disrupt their financial worlds. They have a false sense of security that their paychecks provide every week, which in their minds, justifies their overspending.

Some families have reached the point where they are so financially leveraged that every dollar is spoken for before it is even earned. For these families, all it takes is for one missed paycheck and their whole world is in a complete tailspin, all because one piece of the puzzle failed to come together one month. When you are living this tight, you cannot afford for anything to go wrong in any given month. Everything must come together perfectly. This is not going to happen each month. When debt is around, you gamble and cross your fingers each month, hoping nothing new will go wrong.

Individuals and families who are in debt have failed to ask one important question, as they began to sink deeper and deeper into debt.

CAN I AFFORD THIS?

These are four simple words that should be asked every time a purchase is contemplated. If everyone asked this question and answered it honestly, no one would be in debt.

If you are in debt, go back and look at every big purchase you have made in the last couple of years. If you had truly asked yourself, "Can I afford this item?" what would your financial world look like today?

Families and individuals must wake up and realize that they must be more responsible with their money. Overspending can have severe consequences!

Lives can be more fulfilling and rewarding without the constant drain that debt can have on individuals and families. By spending without a plan and not paying attention to your finances, you are jeopardizing your future.

The decisions you make at the sales counter today are guaranteed to affect your quality of life down the road. If you charge $2,000 worth of Christmas gifts, you will feel the consequences of that purchase in the months to come, possible years. Remember to always ask the question, "Can I afford this?" We will never be able to fully appreciate and live life to the fullest, if we let debt control our minds and our lives. God did not intend for us to live our short lives in debt.

6. Devouring Debt One Step at A Time

Once you have drawn a line in the sand and you are determined to eliminate debt, the process can be agonizingly slow and extremely stressful at times. For some, eliminating debt will be the biggest and most rewarding battle they will ever fight in their lives.
Debt does not just appear out of nowhere! You do not wake up one morning and suddenly realize you are in debt, so you are not going to wake up another morning and suddenly be out of debt. If only it were that easy! Anything in life that is worth something takes effort in achieving; that is why getting into debt is so easy, because it takes absolutely no effort.

Getting out of debt is a process; a process that takes time. In order to conquer debt, you must be in "shape" both mentally and physically to complete a journey to free yourself of the debt. The whole process can seem overwhelming at times, which can cause you to second guess yourself as you would with any monumental task where the rewards are great. So, how does one go about getting out of debt? The way you get out of debt is the same way you get into debt—one step at a time. Remember, it is a process that does not happen quickly.

Hikers, who attempt to walk the Appalachian Trail, focus on completing one day at a time and reaching one shelter at a time, instead of focusing on the entire trail. This enormous 2,181-mile journey through fourteen states is a mind-boggling adventure which takes incredible mental and physical stamina to complete. There are a few who attempt to walk this entire trail and underestimate the endurance it takes to go the distance. The only way for hikers to be successful is to break this journey down into manageable days, so that they are not overwhelmed or overextended. By pushing your body too hard and too fast, you lessen the odds of ever finishing the trail.

As you walk through your own Appalachian trail of debt, you must also anticipate that you will not have the same level of excitement, enthusiasm, sacrifice and mental toughness to combat the debt every week. There will be plenty of highs and lows to deal with each month. The highs will be filled with an incredible sense of accomplishment and the lows will be filled with feelings of doubt, which will make you question if you will ever rid your life of debt. You will also question your own will to cross the finish line, especially when unexpected expenses start to surface which can take some wind from your sails.

When tackling debt, break your journey down into individual manageable months, in order to focus on 30 days at a time. By breaking down this journey into small bites, you will not be so overwhelmed. It is quite easy to get overwhelmed and discouraged if you do not break your goals down to manageable bites. One reason people fail at achieving goals is because the goals they have set are not reachable or realistic, so they burn out quickly having accomplished nothing at all.

When a football team is down by 21 point at halftime, they do not panic and try to get all three touchdowns back in the 3rd quarter. They focus and play hard for the next fifteen minutes and not look ahead to the 4th quarter. Experienced coaches break the game down by quarters and concentrate fifteen minutes at a time. Their focus and concentration need to be on the quarter in which they are playing, so that they can give 100%. By looking ahead, you take your eye off the ball and lose concentration. A receiver, who looks to the end zone before he catches the football, will not gain any yards because he loses focus by taking his eye off the football, causing him to drop the pass.

Remember, when battling debt; expect frustrations because they are coming. Get ready for it, anticipate it and plan for it! Anybody who has accomplished anything in life will tell you that when you set out on a meaningful journey, you will encounter obstacles. Anticipate the obstacles and do your best to work around them. The big three obstacles you will face when trying to become debt free are unexpected expenses, unexpected events, and doubt. Hikers on the Appalachian trail at some point question their endurance and mental toughness to finish. Football teams also privately question whether they have what it takes to measure up and compete against another team. Doubt is something everyone encounters privately, it's human nature.

It is not easy to get out of debt but keeping your eye on the ball and staying focused will eventually get you there. If you could just snap your fingers and make the debt disappear, everyone would do it. It will not happen that way. You must get mad, get off your sofa, get busy and make it happen! The reason you are in debt is because it was easy and effortless.

Imagine for a second what it would feel like, not to have to check in each month with your creditors and send them a percentage of your hard-earned salary. When you are in debt, it can feel as if you are on probation and must check in with your parole officer monthly. Every time you check in late, you are slapped with penalties, in the form of hefty late fees. We get so use to checking in with our creditors each month, we tend to forget what it was like when we were free before debt entered into our life.

Just imagine what it would feel like not to wear that ball and chain that debt so conveniently provides. Reporting every month to your creditors is not the way to be living. The only thing standing between you and your new life is your dirty debt.

Remember, as you work toward your new life by eliminating your debt, staying focused one month at a time is crucial. This will be the key to success. Focus, focus, and more focus. With each month that you sacrifice and endure, you are that much closer to starting your new life without debt. You must keep reminding yourself that you are embarking on this journey so that you can take back the life that debt has quietly stolen from you. This is one journey that is worth crossing the finish line.

7. A LIFE OF CONSTANT STRUGGLE (MARY'S STORY)

As children, we take on the properties of sponges and absorb everything that we see modeled by the environment that surrounds us. We pick up our parents and grandparents' accents and quirky expressions which are freely tossed around the house.

These accents stick with us our entire lives, along with all the family traditions and weird habits that we inherit. We laugh at our parents, when they tell us we are going to be just like them when we get older, but it eventually happens. We end up just like them. They were right!

We learn everything from the environment that we are placed in, from how we communicate to how we dress. We also absorb our parents likes and dislikes when it comes to food and drink. If our parents are coffee drinkers, we will probably become coffee drinkers. If our parents like seafood, there is a great chance we will also like seafood. We will also pick up the less desired tendencies and habits from our parents by default. If our parents use foul or racist language, there is a good chance that we will use foul and racist language. If our parents run a messy and unorganized home, there is a good chance our home will be run the same way. When it comes to money and finance, we learn the good habits and the bad habits of our parents, grandparents, or guardians, as well. Our very first lessons on spending and managing money come from observing how the adults handle household finances.

Let's take Mary for example. A quick snapshot of her finances and her life reveal that it is almost identical to that of her mother and her grandmother. A single mother of

two, making a yearly salary of $17,000 along with child support, helps to make Mary's month come together. This, along with the help of signature loans - (loans that are granted without security) and government assistance, aids in filling in the money gaps along the way.
Mary is living a lifestyle that more resembles a $40k annual income than a $17k annual income.

Struggling financially has always been a part of Mary's family history and will likely remain a part of it, until new ways of handling money are presented. Mary has learned everything she knows about money through her mother and grandmother. These money habits are now being observed and quietly passed down to Mary's own children. By allowing this to happen, Mary is setting the stage for yet another generation of debt to remain in the family tree.

Mary cannot remember a time in her life when payments were not part of any given month. She has become accustomed to the money coming in and going right back out, the very same day. She cannot imagine a month, without payments on loans with high interest rates would be like. In Mary's mind, this is how life is. It is the only world that she has ever known and she seems to be very comfortable and content living within.

Mary and her family are prime targets for companies like pay day loans, pawn shops, rent to own shops and finance companies, all of which charge high interest rates for various loans and merchandise. With a checkered credit history, she is limited as to where she can shop to borrow money and these companies understand that she does not have many choices in her search for credit. They fully understand that for many reasons, they are the only game in town. In Mary's eyes, she must borrow money and refinance loans to survive because she has not been taught any other way to play the personal finance game. Budgeting and saving were never introduced or discussed in the family.

With her checkered payment history on borrowed money, low credit rating and lack of stable employment, Mary is not welcomed by banks. She is, however, more than welcome by the wave of third tier lenders who depend on people like Mary to fuel their business and boost their profits. The people that these businesses attract are people who do not qualify for reasonable interest rates, offered by banks and credit unions. By continually borrowing from these lenders, Mary makes it that much more difficult to ever break free from debt.

In Mary's world, monthly payments are everything. Mary is so caught up in payments that when she shops for loans, she does not inquire about the interest rate, nor is it brought up by the lenders she deals with. She only questions the amount of the monthly payments and signs away. She is not even sure how interest rates are calculated and how they affect the monthly payments.

These third-tier lenders, that welcome Mary and consumers like her, were built on business models created primarily for slow paying customers. These aggressive finance companies expect that a high percentage of their customers will not keep up with their monthly payments. Their projected yearly profits depend heavily on imposing late fees and penalties on customers who are late payers.
Before their loans even become due, borrowers receive aggressive phone calls as reminders that the payment date is approaching. If the account reaches thirty days delinquent, a representative from the loan company is usually sent out to knock on the customer's door to create a sense of urgency

while collecting the payment. Where else in this world can you get great personalized customer service like this?

That is how serious these companies are, when it comes to getting their money back. These companies set an early precedent with their customers, by letting them know that if the payments are not made on a timely basis, they will come to their neighborhood to collect the money.
Usually, after a few payments are made on these high interest loans, the customers can refinance their loans. Most loans are set up for monthly or bi-monthly payments. By pressuring their customers to refinance their loans, the lenders trap the customers into loans which often are never paid off. As long as these loans are on the lender's books, interest is earned every single month. The interest rates are generally exceedingly high because of the effort and expense needed to service theses high risk loans. Once you get snagged in one of these loans, the finance companies make it very difficult for you to walk away.

Not fully understanding how the money game is played is what keeps Mary a prisoner with these types of loan companies. She does not understand the financial terms, credit score or credit worthiness, or the difference between borrowing money at eight or eighteen percent interest. She has never viewed her own personal credit report and is not motivated to do so. She does not understand how important it is to make payments on time, when she borrows money. She figures as long as the finance company gets their money, what's the harm if the payment is late. She does not seem to have a problem paying late fees for the use of the loan company's money. Late fees and disconnect fees are also common with just about every service she has, from her cell phone to her electric bill.

At a young age, Mary inherited special traits and skills on how to deal with debt collectors. Debt collectors calling the house is something that happened daily. So much so, she even knew how to "handle" them at the tender age of eleven. Mary recalls how the kids in the home had to rotate answering the phone in order to "handle" the collectors that called, since her mom was never in the mood to speak to them. She called it "phone duty." "When it was your turn, she said, you had to answer all the calls for the day."

It seemed like most weeks, the phone had been disconnected, so there was no need to worry about collectors calling. When this happened, the collectors would simply call the neighbors and leave messages for the family or simply pay a personal visit in which they were instructed not to answer the door.

The kids were forced to deal with persistent collectors and were sometimes on the receiving end of their abuse. The abuse was a result of pure frustration, because they were never able to reach Mary's mother.

Mary's mother did not want to deal with the collectors because she had no money to give them, so there was no need in talking with them. With no money to throw at the debt, it was the children's job to shield their mother from the angry debt collectors.

Mary's family now has the luxury of caller ID to shield debt collectors, a tool that she did not have access to when it was her turn to answer the phone.

Mary's family dealt with debt by simply not dealing with it. There was never a blueprint floating around the house on how to manage or save money. Wise money management and counsel were non-existent. The money came in and the money went out, in a basic attempt to survive. "We didn't need one of these financial advisors in a fancy suit that you

see on TV helping us manage the money because it didn't hang around long enough to need managing."
Money was something that was hardly ever discussed in Mary's home, because nobody ever had any. According to Mary, "you don't handle something you don't have."

Living below the poverty line was also passed down from the family tree. According to the US Health & Human Services in 2020, the poverty line for a family of three, living in America is $21,720.00

It's not clear if Mary and her children will ever break the cycle of government dependence and high interest rate finance companies. Her mother and grandmother still heavily depend on government assistance as their only source of steady income. There is no real urgency to break out of the dependency lifestyle that Mary is living. She is content with the way things are going in her life.

The desire to improve Mary's life is missing. This is the first crucial step to making a change and gaining financial security. She refuses to believe that she will ever be debt free or even have any money saved. She cannot even begin to entertain or imagine the feeling of financial independence. Mary is too busy struggling to put food on the table to even dream of another kind of life. A life without constant payments to creditors or collection agencies is out of reach for Mary, or at least in her mind, perceived to be out of reach.

It is highly likely that the financial direction in which Mary's life is heading will be passed down to her kids, continuing in the example their mother has set as far as debt and government dependence is concerned. The trend of passing down flawed ways of handling money will probably stretch down to Mary's grandchildren.

Mary does not seem to be in a position or have the desire to teach her children about the correct way to handle money. She cannot teach them what she has not learned herself. Her kids cannot rely on their father's input or knowledge because he is not even in the picture. Therefore, it will be up to Mary to see that her kids are educated on the proper ways to manage and save money.

This family will continue to pass down debt and government dependency from generation to generation unless someone in the family breaks the chains and takes the family in a completely different financial direction.

8. Assessing Your Level of Stress (Ken's foreclosure)

There is no disputing the fact that when debt invades your life, it goes straight to your nervous system and attacks you from a mental and physical standpoint. It is relentless, it never sleeps or takes breaks, it works around the clock, and it will stick around until you ask it to leave.

Debt is something that can weigh heavily on your mind, and it can become a serious issue over time. When you are at the point in your life where problems are hitting you from every direction, you start to question your level of stress and wonder how much you are capable of handling, before you lose it all.

Stress affects people in different ways and must not be overlooked or brushed aside. Debt can easily lead to a state of depression, since it can sometimes seem that there is no way out. The stress of the debt can bring you into dark and lonely places, where your judgment gets clouded, which then opens the door to dark thoughts which can destroy you.

Ken experienced firsthand how financial stress affected him both mentally and physically and forced him to make some tough decisions for his own good and the good of his family.

Ken was facing imminent foreclosure on his home which was six months of payments in arrears. In addition to his past due mortgage was his out of control credit card debt, which was falling further behind with each passing month. The pressure Ken was feeling was starting to affect his mental and physical state of mind to the point where he was having trouble sleeping and getting out of bed in the morning. His production at work had started to decline which grabbed the attention of his boss. He had also started withdrawing from his family which had his wife extremely concerned.

He was steadily losing weight and had abandoned his morning running routine.

With his debt out of control, Ken was taken hostage by the stress that his debt created. The debt was robbing Ken of precious quality time with his wife and children, time that was lost and can never be made up.

Debt is no different from someone holding a gun to your head and controlling your every move. You are being controlled and robbed of your freedom anyway you look at it.

Ken had reached the point where some tough financial decisions had to be made very soon. Does he walk away from the house that his family loves or does he stay and try to fight to keep his house? One thing was for sure, he could not continue to keep living this way, as he was surely headed to an early grave if changes were not made.

He was to the point where he felt that it was impossible to climb out of the financial hole that he had created. The bank was breathing down his neck and was about to foreclose, so a decision had to be made. With the bank closing in on Ken, he attempted to sell his home. Ken owed $20,000 more on his home than what it was currently worth on the open market. This is what the mortgage industry calls, "underwater."

Ken was willing to look at all options; he even considered short selling the home. A short sale occurs when the mortgage holder agrees to accept less than what is owed on the house if a suitable buyer approaches with an offer to purchase. The mortgage company reluctantly agrees to this, in an attempt to avoid having to foreclose on the house. A foreclosure process is very lengthy and costly to any mortgage company and is always avoided if possible.

Ken needed to realize that his house and credit card bills were not worth a mental breakdown. Ken's mental state was at great risk, the longer he hung on to the house.
If walking away from the house and putting his bills on hold would improve his state of mind and keep his family together, then that is what he would do. Ken's family needed him much more than they needed the house. It was more important to Ken's family that he maintains his health rather than keep up house payments.

With no luck attracting buyers for his home, Ken was forced to pack up and walk away from the only home that his children had known. Walking away from the house was the best thing that Ken could have done for his family.

The foreclosure will hurt Ken's credit for years to come but time will eventually correct it. Credit, over time can heal and be rebuilt. Another house will eventually come around and hopefully Ken will be in a much better financial situation and can avoid the mistakes that caused him to lose his current home. The financial scars will be with Ken for a while and will continue to serve as a constant reminder of how debt destroys dreams.

In Ken's case, less turned out to be more. By making the decision to walk away from the house and become a renter. Ken could let go of the stress and reclaim his life. Ken still has a mess to clean that the foreclosure left behind. At least now, he will be able to breathe and think clearly.

With the incredible pressure Ken was under, he kept his priorities in line by walking away from the house. Ken was careless with his spending and for that his family has now paid the price by losing the home.
What is done is done, Ken must let it go and look forward to the future. It is important to know when to walk away and cut your losses.

In the big picture, the house was miniscule compared to his family's security and his wellbeing. Ken's future is bright; he has earning potential. He will recover! He will be smarter! Ken was willing to lose the battle with the home in order to win the war so that his health and sanity could be preserved.

In football, coaches know the importance of knowing when to throw in the towel and pull the starting quarterback out of the game. If the game is a blowout, the coach will not risk injury to his star quarterback, if there is no way the game can be won. The coach is willing to concede this game in hopes of winning more in the future, with his star quarterback in the game. An injured starting quarterback does the team no good.

Similarly, the stress of debt can destroy you mentally and divide your family. Realize that a house is just a house, four walls and a roof, that is all it is and there is no house worth losing your family or your sanity over.

There are no possessions in this world worth holding on to if your health is directly affected by it. Whether it is a boat, car, vacation home, camper, whatever it is, get rid of it, if it is bringing financial stress into your home. Your peace, sanity, and family come first in life before any possessions.

9. The Best Offense is a Good Defense

Any sports fan can tell you that in any sport, offense sell tickets and defense wins games. Every summer thousands of residents who live near the Gulf of Mexico prepare for the worst and hope for the best, as the Atlantic hurricane season gets underway, and runs from June to November, with the peak of the season occurring from August through October.
This is when the Gulf waters are warm and can provide the fuel needed to grow and strengthen hurricanes. Residents prepare for these storms by having sufficient bottled water, batteries, food, and gasoline to run generators. Municipalities put trust in the levee system which is their defense from rising waters.

Unlike hurricanes, financial storms have seasons that run from January through December and give no warning when approaching. They can strike at any time and any place, usually in the form of unexpected emergencies. It is not a matter of if they will strike, but when! So, how do you weather a financial storm? The best way to weather any financial storm is to have a good defensive plan in place, which is your personal levee system. By having no debt and an emergency buffer fund, which can be easily liquidated to contain and quiet any approaching storm, are good levee systems to have in place.

Financial storms come in many shapes and sizes, from medical deductibles to full blown engine replacements. When these storms make landfall, we need to be able to absorb them and make them go away as soon as possible.

This is the job of your emergency buffer fund; to be able to absorb the impact of an emergency. Just as a levee protects a city and a bullet proof vest protect a police officer.

When it comes to finances, you must always plan, prepare, and expect financial storms to hit. Your guard must never be down, and your financial house should always be strong and ready to absorb and weaken even a powerful category five hurricane. By taking a proactive stand, you will always be prepared when financial storms invade your home. There is a certain level of peace and comfort that come with knowing you are prepared in case of financial emergencies.

10. Get Busy Living or Get Busy Dying (The Danger of being Institutionalized)

Get busy living or get busy dying was a phrase used by the character Ellis "Red" Redding played by Morgan Freeman in the classic movie Shawshank Redemption. In the movie, Freeman plays a prisoner who is serving out a life sentence for a murder he committed in his youth. Having served his entire adult life behind bars, Red is referred to as an "institutional man;" meaning he only knows one life, a life behind bars with no freedom and unable to make it on the outside walls of prison if ever granted the opportunity. In prison, the only thing that he has full control over is his mind, he is free to dream and take his thoughts to wherever he wishes.

Once he is paroled, he struggles to find himself in the free world and silently wishes he could break parole so that he could end up back in prison where he is told when to eat, sleep and what to wear. This is the only life he is comfortable living; a life where he is not forced to make any decisions because the institution has already made the decisions.

Now a free man on the outside, he is forced to decide to either get busy living or get busy dying. Living would mean going out and fighting to reinvent and establish a new life in an unfamiliar world, while dying would have meant either going back to prison or taking his own life. The bars that have physically restrained him for years on the inside, now restrain his mind on the outside. With his mind restrained, his future is unclear and hangs in the balance.

When debt is closely examined, it could easily be replaced with prison. In many ways, debt performs the same functions as a prison cell. When you are saddled with debt, you are held prisoner and told by creditors when and how much to pay. If you do not do as you are told, you get slapped with a hefty penalty for not following the rules that the institution has laid out.

When debt has played a dominate role in life, it is easy to become an institutional debtor since you are always being told when and how much to pay. When you get accustomed to receiving monthly statements from creditors, you become oblivious and do not even blink at the outrageous interest being charged. In many cases, the interest is thousands of dollars that is going into the bank accounts of creditors every year.

When we pay off a creditor, we are forced to decide just as Red did to either get busy living in a world without debt or continue dying by supporting our creditors.

Some who have made the decision to pay off their debt so that they could experience freedom, constantly find themselves struggling to remain debt free. Just as it is for a parolee to avoid going back to prison, it is just as hard to remain free of debt and not return to a world of debt. It is a constant battle between the temptation to charge now and pay whenever or to avoid that purchase and remain debt free. Being debt free must be viewed the same way a parolee views being out of prison, a chance at a bright future. Freedom is a wonderful gift and can come in a variety of ways, whether it is freedom from prison, debt, abusive relationships, illnesses or whatever the situation might be.

For many people it is the fear of the unknown that has such a tight grip on their minds that make them unknowingly institutionalized. Once you have reached the point in your life where you are so reliant on "something" that provides a false sense of security and the mere thought of losing it frightens the heck out of you; you have become institutionalized and unable to see clearly.

I interviewed a single mother of two who was in debt and relying strictly on government aid to support her children. This single mother had over the years, become institutionalized by relying on the government to provide her a way of life. By relying on the government to meet her needs for so long, she does not know how she will make it on the outside once her children reach 18 years of age and the checks stop coming.

With the continued reliance on the monthly check from the government, comes a false sense of security that caused her to literally shut down and not attempt to reach her God given potential. This was a very articulate woman with a great personality, no handicaps, or medical issues. She did not work, did not try to improve what skills she already possessed and became content and settled into a life that was provided to her, courtesy of the federal government.

The worse thing that could have happened in this woman's life was to be awarded a monthly check; a check that caused her to give up and lose her way. By receiving the monthly check, she lost the will to fight and to grow so that she could provide the best possible life for herself and her children.

She was selling herself short in a big way by limiting how much living she could do. The government decided how much living this woman was allowed from month to month. She did not fight the decision that was handed down to her. By cashing the check every month, she surrendered to the government. With the checks rolling in, the government controlled her destiny.

Outside employment would have meant a reduction in her monthly check; a path she was not willing to travel down. Relying on the monthly check was being observed by the children, thus paving the way for another generation to follow the same path.

Regardless of how you arrive at being institutionalized, the stakes are enormous and can cause you to adapt and settle into false comfort, where you are unable to find your way out.

11. Can You Afford That Dog? (Charlotte's Story)

As parents, we strive to give our children everything they need and want. In doing so, it is easy to go overboard on purchases. On impulse purchases we often calculated the math in front of the cash register, while holding on to the items we wish to purchase. As we wait for the credit card to be approved, a red or green light subconsciously appears in our heads usually confirming that we may or may not be able to afford the item. We do not factor in the interest involved or the long-term expense, because we rarely consider the future that is tied to the purchase price. We fail to calculate the yearly maintenance costs involved on different items that we invite into our lives. Some purchases have ongoing maintenance costs that extend way beyond the purchase price. Swimming pools, pets and automobiles are purchases that not only have initial costs but recurring costs every year for care and maintenance.

Purchasing pets is no different than purchasing merchandise. Pet costs must be accounted for and worked into the monthly budget. All too often, pets are put in a separate category and are not considered a monthly expense. According to American Pet Products Association, Americans spent an astonishing $72 billion on their furry friends in 2018. That figure represents a lot of maintenance!

When I crossed paths with Charlotte, she was recently forced to decide the fate of a pet that would have lasting effects, both emotionally and financially on her family. Charlotte's dog had been hit by a car and required numerous surgeries to save the dog's life. After consulting with the veterinarian on the cost and with the urging of her family, she elected to go forward with the operations to keep the dog alive instead of putting it to sleep. The grand total was $4,600 for the veterinary care. This amount was charged to a credit card with an 18% interest rate. Which means this expense is hanging around for a while.

This unforeseen veterinary bill was a real blow to the family and one that they were not prepared to handle financially. With this huge expense now a reality, Charlotte and her family are now forced to dig their way out of a much larger financial hole. With the family finances already at a critical stage, this problem just compounds the financial stress.

The dilemma that many families are faced with when expenses must be cut is telling a pet goodbye. Shedding an expense with a heartbeat and a wagging tail is more difficult than shedding material expenses.

When considering the purchase of a pet, it is crucial that you have your financial house in order and consider all the potential expenses. You must consider, all the what if scenarios that could occur, when you invite a dog to be part of the family. By adding a dog to the family, you could literally be looking at thousands of dollars in yearly expenses, especially if the dog gets sick.
In a good year, when expenses are just food and veterinary checkups, you are still looking at substantial expenses.
Any pet owner will tell you that from an expense standpoint, pets are no different than a child. In some cases, families are forced to make decisions between the financial stability of the family or re-homing the pet. Every pet owner needs to know where to draw the line as far as expenses are concerned.

Charlotte admits that she could not afford the dog in the first place, as they were already reaching the end of the money before the month was over. They were not actively looking to purchase, but once her children stumbled into the pet store and held the dog for the first time, there was no going back.

Obviously, the dog did not single handedly expose this family financially. The dog simply was the exclamation point which magnified and exposed an already poor financial situation.

This family can recover with a strong game plan in place for their money. They must be willing to know when to say when, concerning pet expenses in the future, however cruel that might sound.

Family needs always come first, especially before pets. If Charlotte's dog can serve as a wakeup call for this family and get them to manage and budget their money more effectively, perhaps some good can come out of this misfortune! When we last spoke to Charlotte, her dog was fully-recovered and she had managed to cut expenses in other areas in order to accommodate the addition of the dog.

12. Dating or Paying Off Debt

In the world of dating, the questions that have traditionally been asked over the years, when trying to find a suitable match are, does he or she have kids? Are they smokers? What do they do for a living? How much money do they make? Are they tall or short?

The additional questions that have now surfaced are more geared towards one's financial status. What is their fico score? How much do they make? Have they ever filed bankruptcy? Do they have a gambling problem? How the world's views have shifted over the years. People are getting more and more selective on who they date, and financial profiles play a big role. Today, people are hesitant to enter relationships where debt has an overwhelming presence. Most people today are looking for easy and convenient relationships that flow and do not come with a lot of drama or hassle. This is especially true for people just coming out of relationships.

So how do you enter in the world of dating with debt?

Having debt makes it extremely tough to wine and dine without going further into debt. Most will continue to rack up debt as they feel it is more important to find that special someone than to pay down debt. Dating is not cheap and takes money, this is money that people in debt do not have at their disposal.

On the other hand, some people are just so disgusted with their financial situation that they elect to just remove themselves altogether from the world of dating so that they can avoid the embarrassment. They become prisoners in their own home, too embarrassed to venture out.

They become dejected and lonely because they have no financial freedom to do anything worthwhile. They convince themselves that it is safer to stay hidden and out of sight, than to potentially be exposed and ridiculed once the truth comes out about their financial woes.
We see this especially, in the thirty to forty age group. Most people in this age group are coming out of marriages with debt. This poses a big problem, when you are saddled with debt and trying to re-engage or stay in the dating game in hopes of establishing a long-term relationship.

These people want desperately to date but are truly in bondage due to the debt they carry. Not being able to take part in dating can be very depressing and lonely for many as they feel life is passing them by without being able to fully participate. They feel they are not getting any younger and truly desire to be in a meaningful relationship, while still in the prime of their lives.

Debt is one of the first major hurdles that must be overcome, for a relationship to advance. For many, it is too big of a hurdle to clear. Once the debt issue is visited, two things are bound to happen; stick around or flee. The ones that flee will feel that the debt is just too big of a hurdle and move on. These are the individuals who are usually in better financial shape and would rather find someone more financially compatible. The ones that stick around feel that their relationship is deeper than the debt and eventually the debt can be overcome and tamed. These individuals usually are more financially compatible and at one point have probably had to deal with debt and are more sympathetic towards it.

If you are in a relationship and debt has not been discussed, you know that it is not a question of if it will be discussed, but when will it be discussed. In the back of your mind, you know that question is coming, and you dread the day, especially if you are guilty of carrying debt. You are also aware that the debt can shift the direction of relationships and play a huge role in determining the future. The shame and embarrassment that debt carries cannot be avoided and must be dealt with eventually, when entering relationships that have potential.

When is a good time to bring up the topic of debt? You certainly do not want to bring it up over dinner on the first date. That will surely guarantee that a second date will not take place.

You might feel that if you can buy time in order to avoid the debt issue, while continuing to pour on the charm until love surfaces, then the debt issue might somehow be minimized and go over smoother, when brought up for discussion.

Timing is extremely important, when bringing up the topic of debt. You do not want to bring it up too early and you do not want to bring it up too late in a relationship. You need to lay it out, on the table, once you both agree that there might be potential for the relationship to take off.

You certainly do not want to bring it up, after you have set a date to get married and the wedding invitations have been ordered.

With online dating now a household word, you are now able to shop and choose the particulars, you are looking for in a mate. Unlike the traditional ways of finding dates, online match making services can provide you with many personal details including, geographical preferences along with the desired height and weight, with the latter ones sometimes being exaggerated.

Online dating services often provide you with desired income levels to aid in your search for a suitable mate, but nowhere does it mention on profiles the levels of debt that one might have.

So, why is the question, how much debt do you have, asked? Is it a valid question? You bet! The top reason for divorce is finances and debt. Most people coming out of a failed marriage can attest to the fact that it is a major problem. That is why single and divorced people that are dating, ask this question. They know that debt can lead to serious marital problems.
Most that have been in relationships filled with debt are not willing to travel down that road again. Marriages starting out are tough enough to navigate and when you throw in debt, it makes it even tougher for a marriage to succeed. If the focus is on debt and not each other, a marriage will have a hard time taking off, much less grow and flourish.

Statistically, there is a good chance that if you are dating, you might meet someone that is in debt. Are you prepared to fall in love with someone that does have debt? If you are then you must find the root of the problem to determine what caused that person to go into debt, in the first place. By hanging out and observing your potential mate's spending habits and tendencies, you should then be able to get a good picture of their true nature. If you do decide to go forward and eventually marry, you are also marrying the debt and the debt will be accompanying you on the honeymoon. With that said, is the love that you have for each other stronger than any amount of debt? These are valid questions that must be addressed before you say I do. Collectively come together and iron out a plan to eliminate the remaining debt. Working together to eliminate the debt could be an opportunity to bond and strengthen the relationship.

Do not let debt alone, determine if you will go forward or not in a relationship. Try not to prejudge an individual just because debt is part of the picture. By not going forward, you might be missing out on the love your life. On the other hand, you might be saving yourself from a marriage destined for a divorce because of finances. Make sure you look at the whole picture and examine all the variables that went into accumulating the debt. Always try to rely on your gut instinct and prayers when searching for guidance in relationships.

13. Retaliatory Spending (Mark & Terri's Story)

To say that marriages are a walk in the park and take absolutely no effort to keep them going would be a huge exaggeration. Marriages are just the opposite and take an incredible amount of energy and often face numerous obstacles, with debt and finances being one of the biggest challenges a marriage can face.
Debt can be introduced or accumulated in a marriage in several ways. One-way debt finds its way into a marriage is through retaliatory spending. With this type of spending, couples fight without getting physical. By charging and running up debt, they are showing their discontent towards their spouse, while digging a big financial hole in this winless battle of "I will show him," or "I will show her."
Retaliatory spending occurs in a marriage when one spouse fires the first shot in the form of a major purchase without the other spouse's knowledge or support. To get revenge, the other spouse fires back with a purchase of equal or greater value, just to prove a point and to level out the playing field.

With the first round of shots fired, two things are bound to happen in this spending frenzy. The spending will either cease after the angry spouse retaliates and the marriage resumes back to a somewhat normal state or both parties will continue to fight until the spending gets way out of control.

Either way the marriage takes a harmful blow the amount of debt incurred during the storm will usually determine the recovery time it takes for the marriage to get back to normal. The debt will linger around in the marriage if steps are not taken to eliminate it. By allowing the debt to hang around after the fight, you will have constant reminders of the new debt which could invite opportunities for bickering to flare up.

When one spouse plans to make a major purchase without the consent of the other spouse, their individual income likely plays a major role in determining whether they go forward with the purchase or not. When one spouse earns most of the family's income and feels that this enables them to spend freely, friction is bound to occur in the marriage. By not consulting with your spouse on a major purchase, you are sending messages that the relationship is not 50/50 and that your spouse's thoughts or concerns are not important in the relationship. When one spouse feels left out of the family's financial decisions because of income inferiority, a split in the marriage has occurred. Income inferiority occurs when one spouse feels they have less of a voice, because of their individual earnings contribution

In Mark and Terri's case, the bickering started when Mark came home with the purchase of a new bass boat. Mark had always dreamed of one day owning a boat and entering in regional bass tournaments, so with the purchase, he was one step closer to realizing his dreams.
Unfortunately for Mark, Terri did not share in his dreams especially the part which puts the family in debt over a boat. Terri was extremely angry with Mark after making such a huge purchase without consulting her. She felt slighted and betrayed, as if her opinion did not matter and was terribly upset over the purchase. She did not understand why her husband needed a new boat to enter fishing tournaments, since the old boat worked simply fine and was paid for.

Terri became even more enraged when Mark refused to discuss the purchase. When questioned further, Mark shouted that he works hard and earns most of the family income and that he deserved a new boat and did not need anyone's permission to buy it. With Mark's statement, the first shot in the upcoming spending war had been fired.

Two days later, Terri surprised Mark with a purchase of her own, a brand-new car. She had traded in her old car for a new one at a local car dealership. When Mark questioned her about it, she simply replied that since she works hard, she also deserved to be driving around in style; the style that only a new car could offer.

Mark was clearly upset but realized that he had no comeback and was out of ammunition, since he used it all on defending the purchase of his boat. He realized that his actions had set this whole storm in motion and could possibly end up jeopardizing the marriage.

Within a one-week period, the couple increased their debt load by $61,000 ($28,000 for the boat and $33,000 for the car). This was $61,000 that was not even planned for or even slightly discussed but is now a part of their marriage. After a couple of days had passed, the couple had a chance to calm down and breathe. They realized how foolish and hasty they had acted and reacted without even consulting each other. The couple's debt load went from $25k to $86k which represented a 244% increase within a seven-day period.

These purchases have now changed Mark and Terri's entire financial landscape and could have serious implications on their future, especially if they are forced to deal with any unexpected expenses in the future.

Their debt to income ratio had increased dramatically within a short time period. They will now be forced to reassess and prioritize their finances now that a new car and boat are part of the equation.

Finances are the number one reason people get divorced, so engaging in retaliatory spending is extremely dangerous for a marriage.

When couples act out and show their displeasure in the form of overspending there are usually greater underlying problems in the marriage that need to be addressed. The newly accumulated debt just brings on added stress and greater consciences to a marriage. By overspending we sometimes try to cover up or medicate whatever pain or problems we are experiencing at the time.

When two people are joined in marriage, they should become one entity in everything they accomplish or engage in. A true marriage should be two equal halves with equal voting rights on every issue. If a marriage is to be successful, it must be an equal partnership, regardless of income, social status, or race.

14. Martin's Grand Plan

Everyone at some point in their life has dreamed about becoming self-employed and owning their own business. This feeling is especially magnified when things are not going well at work. We quietly question whether we have what it takes to be a successful business owner. Being the boss, able to call the shots and taking off whenever you want is priceless and sounds great, but does it really work like that? Does being self-employed come with a price tag? You bet! That price tag is unbelievable hard work and dedication. Not to mention, sleepless nights, self-employment taxes, insurance, start-up costs, etc.

Martin was one who had trouble getting thoughts of being self-employed out of his mind. Martin worked for Madison Specialty Products for nearly 25 years and was considered a highly skilled master craftsman and one of the best in the entire industry. Madison Specialty Products was family owned with about 17 employees. Martin took great pride in his work and found it rewarding. His hand-crafted doors were shipped all over the world. He was easily considered the MVE (most valuable employee) of his company, year after year.

Opening his own business had been a dream of Martin's for some time. He figured with the skills he possessed, along with his reputation and contacts in the industry, it would be a smooth transition going from employee to business owner. But the security that his job offered kept his dreams in check. Martin dreamed of someday being closer to his children and opening his own specialty wood company. He and his wife were both 53 years old and in great physical shape so health issues would not stand in the way of him pursuing his lifelong dream of becoming self-employed. As time went on, it got harder and harder for Martin and his wife to tell his children and grandchildren goodbye after visiting on holidays and wished they could see them more often.

Meanwhile, Mr. Madison, the owner of MSP, had suddenly died. His children were engaged in an ugly battle to see who would control the family business. The fighting eventually landed the heirs in court, where a judge would be forced to decide the fate of the employees along with the company. The future of Madison was in real jeopardy.
Martin feared that when it was all said and done, the company would be chopped up and liquidated to settle the lawsuit. Martin was not fond of reporting to the Madison children; he cringed at the mere thought of it. He would quite frequently refer to them as ungrateful little brats who never worked a hard day in their lives. Many of the workers shared Martin's sentiments towards the Madison children. Some of the workers feared the worst and started searching for new jobs, while the battle for control of the company played out in the courtroom.

With all the uncertainty surrounding the company and a burning desire to be closer to his family, Martin had decided one night that now was the time to make the move and start his own business. Regardless of the outcome in court, he was not about to stick around and take orders from those brat children he despised.

With Martin and his wife currently renting an apartment, they would not have the hassle of putting a house up for sale or sticking around until it sold. Martin's wife was a certified elementary teacher so finding work would not be a problem. Nothing was holding Martin and his wife back. They were free to begin the next chapter of their lives.

Martin began to assess his finances and attempted to lay out a financial game plan to get his dream ready for launch. Martin knew one stumbling block that might slow him down was his credit history.

Martin's credit had been on the mend for the last couple of years and was slowly improving and heading upward now that he had some distance between him and a foreclosure which took place several years earlier. Martin's total life savings was comprised of $16,000 in a savings account and $22,000 in an Individual Retirement Account. As far as his debt was concerned, he owed $5,500 on a credit union signature loan which was paid down from $10,000.

Martin had decided that he would secure credit lines and loans to cover the initial startup costs of the new business. He figured that it would not take long to turn a profit because of his contacts in the industry. He also figured that if his former company were liquidated by the courts, as he fully expected, the current customers would be in the market for a new supplier. He also figured that once the banks would see his business model and profit projections, securing loans would not be a problem even with his past bankruptcy. His target customers would be homebuilders who had more business than they could handle. This was due to a boom in construction taking place in the red-hot region of the country where Martin was relocating.

Martin and his wife had planned to purchase a home instead of renting, since that was where they had planned on retiring. The couple began hunting for a home in which they could spend the rest of their lives in. They settled on a house that sat on a ridge which overlooked a pond. Martin especially like the house, because it came with a huge work garage that had unlimited possibilities. The mortgage company was requiring that all their savings be applied to the down payment due to the past foreclosure and credit problems. Martin's wife also had to secure a full-time teaching job before they could be considered for the loan. She had no problem finding work as a certified teacher in this "red hot" area of the country, which had a desperate need for qualified teachers. Along with the teaching salary came the much-needed health insurance benefit which was dropped once Martin left Madison Specialty Products.

With the entire savings going towards the down payment of the new home, the only money they had to their names was the $22,000 IRA. Martin's wife's salary would have to support the family, while he turned his attention to getting his new business up and running.

With the closing of the new home wrapped up and Martin's wife now working, he immediately began to search for a warehouse. Martin located one about 15 miles from his home that seemed to be a perfect fit for the vision he had. The owner of the warehouse was demanding that a five-year lease be signed, in exchange for a discounted monthly rate. Martin figured he was in this venture for the long run, so a five-year lease was not out of the question and did not really bother him. Martin withdrew the deposit for the warehouse along with three months' rent out of his IRA mutual fund. Unfortunately, it came with a hefty penalty for taking out the money before age 59.

He next turned his attention to the bank, in order to secure a much-needed line of credit, so that he could purchase the necessary inventory that was needed to get the venture rolling. According to his own calculations, Martin should have no problem being approved for the $50,000 loan that he was seeking. This money would be used to build up inventory and purchase some initial start-up equipment. Again, he was relying on his reputation and business plan to achieve this.

To his surprise, Martin learned that he was turned down by the bank on the $50,000 loan request, even after presenting his business plan to the bank vice-president. He was approved for a smaller $25,000 loan which he gladly accepted. He figured he would just have to make it work with the smaller loan.

Martin worked like crazy to get his business off the ground and running. He worked the phone lines and made in person sales calls on businesses that were within driving distance. Martin targeted all the high-end homebuilders in the area. He also contacted all his old business associates to let them know he was available and open for business.

Martin rarely saw his wife as he worked almost every weekend getting the business launched. Within the second month of operation, some small orders started to roll in, mostly for custom wood doors. Martin wasted no time on the orders that came in. He hustled to get the orders completed and delivered on time. He was limited in the delivery of his products because his pickup truck could only accommodate a couple of doors at a time which caused him to spend more time on the road.

As Martin's business contacts grew, so did the orders. He began to see repeat orders from one of the biggest homebuilders in county, Smith Custom Homes.

One day, a surprising order was placed by Smith Custom Homes for 155 custom wood doors. This was good news and bad news for Martin. He did not have the inventory in stock or the manpower at the time to handle this massive $60,000 order. That did not deter Martin from accepting it. To accommodate the work, Martin would have to go back to the bank to get a loan to purchase the inventory needed

to complete the order. With Most of Martin's invoices not payable for 60-90 days, he did not currently have the needed cash flow available to make the purchase on his own. The building industry was notorious for being slow in paying invoices and Martin was aware of this.
When one company is slow in paying an invoice to another company, the company waiting to be paid is slow in paying another company. When this happens, you get a trickle-down effect from one company to another. This affects smaller companies greater than it affects larger companies who do not even blink if an invoice is past due.

The next morning, Martin headed to the bank to secure the $60,000 loan needed to fulfill the Smith order. With his fingers crossed, he walked in the bank. Again, to Martin's surprise, his loan request was rejected by the bank. He even showed the loan officer the purchase order from Smith Custom Homes, who the bank knew quite well and had dealings with. Smith Custom Homes used the same bank. The bank still did not budge from their initial decision to decline the loan. For the loan to be approved, the bank required a co-signer on the note, and it could not be Martin's wife. Martin did not know where to turn for help. He knew that this order could really propel his business and get it to a new level, if only he could get the much-needed financing secured. Martin was determined not to let this order slip away. He racked his brains trying to come up with a solution so that the order would not be lost.

Then it hit him. Martin recalled his brother-in-law, Johnny saying over dinner, that they should go into business together and become partners. Martin was about to find out just how serious Johnny was about entering into a partnership. Without his wife's knowledge, Martin contacted Johnny and pitched the proposition.

After a meeting with Johnny to lay out the business plan, Johnny agreed to co-sign the $60,000 personal loan. Johnny was two years away from retiring as a truck driver. He had been with the same trucking company for 30 years and was looking forward to transitioning into a different career. With the stroke of a pen, Johnny & Martin became official partners as their relationship took on a new dimension now that they were both responsible for the loan.

Martin agreed to make Johnny a 20% silent owner of the company. No paperwork was ever drawn up to show this, however. The partnership was simply formed with a handshake and a smile. After all, they are family.

Martin worked long and crazy hours on the Smith order. On some days he could not tell you what day it was and some nights he would work around the clock with no sleep. Martin hardly spent any time at his new home except to eat and sleep. His wife would refer to him as her roommate because she hardly saw him. The Smith order was taking a heavy toll both on Martin's mind and body. At times, he questioned his decision to become a business owner, but figured this is what every business owner must go through in order to get a company off the ground and running.

With the work orders rolling in at a steady pace, Martin figured he needed to invest in a delivery truck because his personal truck could not keep up with the deliveries that had to be made. On some deliveries he was forced to rent a truck in order to save time on the road. In Martin's eyes, this was a wasted expense and figured it was time to have his own delivery vehicle. He figured it would be good for business to have his company name in big bold print spread across a shiny new delivery truck. This would be very prestigious and provide great advertising, which could help pay for the truck.

The next big hurdle was to get Johnny on board with his idea so that he would cosign for the truck loan. Martin explained to Johnny that a new truck could cut the delivery time in half, allowing more productivity. Reluctantly, Johnny agreed after Martin persuaded him that they were on the verge of great things beginning to take shape. Martin informed Johnny that as a 20% owner of the company, there were going to be expenses. Martin explained that this is how companies operate; you must spend money in order to make money. After a quick trip to the bank, Martin drove back to the warehouse in his new $53,000 delivery truck. All that was missing was a sign displaying his company name.

As time went on, Martin had his good days and his bad days. He was surprised as to how many different hats he would be required to wear as a business owner. He did everything from sweeping the floors to shaking hands with top executives. One hour, he was making sales calls, the next hour he was sanding down doors or reconciling invoices.
He often felt so stretched that he could not focus on one thing at a time and that just drove Martin crazy. One evening as he sat alone in his warehouse, he began to think back on the last three years that had just flown by.

He realized that he hardly spends any quality time with his wife, and he did not see his children and grandchildren very much. After all, the children and grandchildren were the primary reason for the move in the first place. Ironically, Martin got to see his children and grandchildren more when he lived five hundred miles away.

During his first year in business, Martin just about broke even, which was below his expectations. Even though Martin did not make any money the first year in business, he was proud of his accomplishments. He often wondered how much longer he would be able to keep up this insane schedule. His second and third year in business showed promise, as steady increases in sales continued.

Martin constantly felt tired and drained and had trouble sleeping some nights with all the pressure he carried. He thought about hiring an apprentice but that would cut into his profit margin. Martin's profit margin wasn't as great as it should be because of the high amount of debt that the company carried.

At times, he silently wished that he was back at his old job, without all these new pressures he had to deal with as an owner. He still loved what he was doing for a living but just did not like the managing of money aspect of the business. Martin missed his wife and the simple life he once knew and enjoyed. He wished he could take a two-week vacation, but that was not going to happen. He could hardly afford to miss a day without getting behind on work.

He was in too deep with the bank to even begin to think about cutting back his hours. Martin needed to do a certain amount of sales just to service the debt that was now on the books. This made the option for time off non-existent.

He enjoyed having his own company but wondered if it was worth the price tag that came with it. He was now 56 years old and starting to question how many quality years of living he had left. Martin felt as if his quality of life was on a steady decline with the amount of time his company demanded of him. He felt as if the business had already stolen three years of his life that should have been spent with his wife, children, and grandchildren. Martin did not own the company. The company owned Martin and it was becoming clearer with each passing month.

Over time, as sales increased, so did the outstanding receivables with more and more slow paying customers surfacing each month. Martin was increasingly spending more of his time on the phone and in person trying to get a handle on his past due receivables. He had a total of $60,000 billed to his customers. This was creating a tremendous strain on his cash flow. The only funds that Martin could access was the money in his IRA mutual fund, which was now down to about $12,000. He was not about to take any more out of that fund. He also was not about to ask his brother-in-law to sign for another loan, not that he would sign for one anyway.

Martin repeatedly wished that he did not have to deal with the money part of this business and could just focus on crafting the doors, but the finances of the business needed serious attention.
To make matters worse, $45,000 of the $60,000 owed to Martin's company was from Smith Custom Homes. SCH started out paying invoices within two weeks of receiving them and then suddenly started paying slower and slower. There was talk floating around the industry that Smith Homes was being sued in a huge class action suit for building on an old hazardous waste site. When Martin heard this news, he got on the phone with their accounting department, which assured him that his check for the whole $45,000 was in line to be processed for payment.

After a couple of months had passed, the orders started to slow down but the receivables were higher than ever. Martin was forced to start demanding cash on delivery with certain customers. He knew this was a risky move and could hurt his business, but he had absolutely no choice in the matter. Martin needed his cash flow to seriously improve or his company would be in big trouble. Without steady cash flow, Martin was having trouble meeting his own monthly obligations. According to several builders, new home purchases were down dramatically. Some long-time builders claim to have never seen such a sudden drop off in work.

As Martin began to focus on his outstanding receivables, he began to get nervous because the Smith check still had not arrived in the office. The last time Martin had spoken with Smith's accounting department, they assured him the check was being processed. The problem this time, according to Smith's accounting office, was a mix up on a purchase order number, but that had been resolved. That was three weeks ago! Martin thought surely the check should have been cut by now. Smith Custom Homes had a great reputation for paying their bills. They had offices in ten states; surely, they had the money to pay a $45k invoice.

Martin picked up the phone to make another call to Smith Homes and the phone number was disconnected. His heart dropped to the floor as he hurried and redialed the number hoping that he had misdialed, but the same disconnected recording came on. By now his worst fears were confirmed; the number was indeed disconnected. He jumped in his truck and drove almost 100 miles to Smith's local office and found the parking lot completely empty of cars. With his heart racing, he parked his truck and slowly made his way to the main entrance. A sign on the door referred all calls to a law firm which was located out of state.

Martin had reached the lowest point since he had started the business. His company was not in a financial position to absorb a $45,000 loss. In fact, it was not able to absorb any amount of loss. Martin realized how foolish it was to leverage that type of transaction on one customer, regardless of the size of the customer. He now realized that he was betting the future of his company on one invoice and on one company's reputation. Martin, along with Johnny took out a personal loan just to accommodate that order. Martin wondered what type of business owner takes out a personal loan just to fill one order. An inexperienced one, he thought! Martin's self-confidence was at an all-time low and concluded he had no business being self-employed. With most of his money tied up in receivables, he did not know how he would be able to pay his bills. The Smith Homes debacle seemed to represent the final nail in the coffin. This seemed to confirm any uncertainty that was remaining in Martin's mind. He closed his office early out of frustration and just went home. This was the first time in nearly three and a half years Martin had gone home early. Two weeks later, Martin received an official notice from the law firm representing Smith Homes. The company was now in chapter 7 bankruptcy protection and in the process of liquidating all its assets. Unfortunately, he was at the bottom of a long list of creditors that needed to be paid. He knew the money was lost.

From that point forward, things just got progressively worse for Martin. The housing industry that Martin relied on so heavily was literally on life support. Record foreclosures were happening all over the country and the economy now had everyone's full attention as it slowly started to sink to unprecedented levels. New construction had come to a complete stand-still. Nobody was building new homes because the demand was simply drying up along with the economy. This meant that no builders had any funds to pay their bills. Some long-time home builders were closing and going into other industries altogether.
By this time, the bank had started calling both business partners, with the loans now falling past due. Martin began

to think if only he had planned better, he might have been able to weather the economic storm that the entire country was in. Martin realized that his debt load was the biggest problem not the slowing of orders. With the amount of debt, he carried it was nearly impossible to weather the financial turmoil he was facing. The pressure for a new business to succeed is great by itself, but by adding debt to the equation, it is almost impossible to succeed when bumps in the road are encountered. New startup companies that carry debt are a catastrophe waiting for the right bump in the road to happen.

With the remaining receivables trickling in slower and slower and sales virtually non-existent, there was no cash flow and no money to pay on the bank loans or the truck loan. With all the events that had unfolded in the last couple of months, Martin and Johnny were not even speaking to one another. Martin's wife had to act as a mediator and messenger between Martin and her brother.

Martin had already turned in the truck to the bank and had agreed to liquidate his IRA to bring current the loans, so that the bank would not go forward with legal action against him.

The bank also agreed not to go after Johnny, so long as the loans remained current. It was now up to Martin and his wife to keep the loans from further default. Martin's landlord was kind enough to allow payment through the end of the year and would forgive the remaining two years on the contract.

According the U.S. Bureau of labor statistics, most failures of new businesses happen within four years of their existence. Only 66% of new businesses make it past the two-year mark and after four years, there are only 44% of new companies still open.

Although Martin was dejected and depressed, he also felt a sense of relief that this burden was lifted from him. Obviously, he had wished the circumstances had unfolded differently, but what is done is done. His biggest regret was removing himself from his family for the past three and a half years. That was more painful than the loss he had just experienced with the business. Martin hardly got to see his children and grandchildren because he was working nearly eighty hours a week. His relationship with Johnny will probably never fully recover, to what it was prior to opening the business. Time does have a way of healing things, especially broken relationships, but this one may not. What started out as a grand plan to move closer to his family while opening a business turned out to be a painful business and life lesson.

Martin wanted so badly to be in business for himself that he failed to come up with a solid plan and properly map out all the expenses. His business plan was hastily put together in a couple of weeks, instead of years of planning. He did not have enough money saved and had to start out borrowing right away, which added pressure to an already pressure-packed situation. Businesses benefit greatly by having the least amount of pressure to deal with, so that they can remain focused on their business models, especially startup businesses.

15. MARTIN FINDS PEACE (GOD'S PRESENCE)

After closing his company and turning in his deliver truck to the bank, Martin then moved all his remaining equipment into his workshop behind the house. Martin immediately began to solicit his contacts that were still alive in the industry, in hopes of finding some type of employment. Martin was not in a position to be picky; he just needed a paycheck. The builders left standing after the economic downturn were the ones that had minimal or no debt on their books and managed their accounts receivable very tightly.

After a couple of months of searching, Martin received a call from Ricky Jones, one of his old customers who was still open for business despite the hard times. Ricky Jones from R.B Jones Construction called to offer Martin an independent contracting position with his company.
Mr. Jones was one of the few builders left standing after the housing industry hit rock bottom. Most of the other companies either consolidated with other companies or simply went out of business. With the building industry still suffering, Ricky had turned his focus to doing home remodels. Mr. Jones had always been impressed with the quality of Martin's work along with his professionalism and prompt delivery of his products, and figured Martin would be a great asset to his company.

Mr. Jones offered Martin a job on a contract basis designing and crafting doors for his company. Best of all, Martin could perform the jobs from his work shed located behind his house which already stored some of his equipment.

Martin never imagined how valuable that shed would become. He knew there was a reason he fell in love with it the minute he saw the house. The necessary products and materials for the jobs would be supplied by R.B Jones Construction, and he would only charge Jones for his labor. There would be minimal out of pocket expenses for odds and ends, but many of the expenses would be handled by R.B. Jones.

This was a perfect set up in Martin's eyes. This was exactly what he needed after experiencing the closing down of his business. Within a week, Mr. Jones had dropped off lumber and supplies to craft six custom doors. Martin immediately started to work on the doors and finished the project two days ahead of schedule. Martin found it rewarding to be doing the work that he was cut out for and not have the pressure that his last failed business venture provided.

He felt so refreshed and fortunate to be in the position he was in. He felt as though he was given a second chance at the work he enjoyed. Word slowly began to circulate that Martin was doing contract work for R.B. Jones Construction and before long he was approached by two smaller builders with proposals. Martin was careful not to overextend himself and limited his work to only nine hours per day something he had not done in the past couple of years of being self-employed. The market was still slow, so he did not have to worry about being overloaded, at least in the immediate future.
Martin was able to perform these jobs without having the overhead of a warehouse, supplies, or his fancy delivery truck, three big expenses Martin was glad to be doing without. Without having to meet big expenses each month, Martin did not have to produce as many doors to make a profit. With less debt to service, he did not have to work as hard.

Martin was able to witness firsthand how destructive debt could be as it slowly took over his world and tarnished his relationship with Johnny. He now knows that without debt, better receivables management, and better planning, his company could have made it through the tough times the same way that R.B. Jones Construction weathered the storm.

Looking back, Martin realized the mistakes he made by rushing his plans to go into business. His plan to move closer to his children and start a company was hatched in a matter of weeks, while the fate of his old company was being played out in court. Martin made a series of mistakes getting his business off the ground. He failed to have the necessary capital to start the business and immediately went into debt to get it going. By not having access to capital, Martin was forced to involve Johnny in order to secure loans. This was not initially part of his hurried plan. He was then forced to tap into his IRA and incur penalties for early withdrawals, which he had not planned on doing either. Another crucial mistake he made was securing the loan that funded the giant Smith Homes order. There was a good reason the bank was not impressed with the Smith order. They knew of the financial problems Smith Custom homes were experiencing but could not disclose them. Martin clearly saw that his plan was not very well thought out. His business plan resembled one that was more along the lines of "go with the flow and improvise along the way." Having debt in the business opened the door and paved the way for unnecessary stress to be ushered into Martin's life. The debt factor is an undisputable game changer and adds a whole new element to the equation, when attempting to launch a new business or simply just managing a household. With Martin's newfound blessings, he was able to eventually pay off all the bank loans that were incurred by his business.

Martin was finally at peace with himself and felt completely fulfilled with the direction that his life was taking. He was now able to visit with his children and spend quality time with them on a regular basis. He enjoyed teaching his grandchildren about the basics of wood working and attending their sporting events. He especially enjoyed just being with his wife and taking walks in the evening after supper. His new contract job provided him with freedoms, that in the past, he could only dream of having. The freedom Martin was now experiencing was priceless and he was never going to trade that for anything in the world.

Martin is thankful to God for allowing him to experience the hardships that he had endured during the past three years as a business owner. This storm humbled him and has made Martin a stronger, wiser, and more appreciative man.

Martin believed God intended for him to be closer to his children and provided him with a path filled with valuable lessons, so that he could grow stronger as an individual and realize the important things in life. Having experienced what he had, Martin realized how going into debt was living in bondage and was not worth sacrificing his life or his family just to fulfill a dream of becoming a business owner.

As time went on, Martin's relationship with Johnny healed and grew stronger. Martin made sure that Johnny did not lose any money during their short "partnership" and realized how cosigning almost brought down the family. Martin continues to enjoy life and thanks God every day for the blessings in his life. Martin has also expanded his work force by adding a part-time helper. You guessed it, Johnny.

If you find yourself in a financial bind and see no way out, it is important to realize, as Martin did, that we are only human and limited physically and mentally as to what we are capable of handling on our own. We need the security, comfort, wisdom, and guidance that only God can provide. If we are relying on man to fill our needs and not God, we will be let down time and time again.

Try giving everything to God. Surrender all your problems to Him, so that He can lighten your load. Nothing is too big for our God to handle. Allow Him into your homes, your families, and your finances.

Having the comfort that God provides will also change how you prioritize things in your life. This will allow you to focus on the gifts God has given you, so that you can apply them in a meaningful way to help others and to bring others to God. As long as you're living on earth you will always face adversity. Only God can supply the strength and peace you need to take on your problems.

16. The Critical Role of Peace - Trusting God Until the End

Finding peace, is a very crucial part of the puzzle, when you are on a journey of a lifetime to rid your life of debt. Whether it is a debt journey or any journey, if you are not at peace with yourself, your journey will be a rocky one, filled with doubt, uneasiness, and a lot of bumps along the way. Having the peace in your soul is what will keep you strong and focused when you encounter tough days along your journey. The peace in your life is the medicine that calms the restlessness in your heart. As the peace grows and the restlessness fades, your convictions become stronger and you can focus more intently on your goals with less distractions getting in the way.
Anyone who is or has been in debt at some point in their lives has imagined a debt free life. Not everyone is able to find the peace that it takes to finish the journey to become debt free, so they come up short.

When you have been beat up by debt for long periods, you start to believe that there is no way out of this trap. You manage to convince yourself that this is how it will always be. You will always live paycheck to paycheck! There will always be more month than money, so what is the use in even trying to get out of debt?

People who have been stung the hardest by debt and have experienced financial pain have a greater desire to find peace. It only takes one believer in the family, to light the fuse that instills hope and changes the entire direction, attitude and focus of the family. The dream has a great chance of succeeding, once the entire family is on board. Three quarters of the battle to conquer debt is changing the family's lifestyle and attitude. Therefore, peace is so important. Without peace, the lifestyle and attitudes will not stand a chance.

To stay on course and eliminate debt, you must be at complete peace with your new changes as they occur. This is the only way you will succeed and permanently stay out of debt. You must be willing to let go and say goodbye to your old lifestyle, even if it means letting go some friends that will hinder your progress. If it means staying away from the department stores and fancy electronic stores, then do not go near them to avoid the temptation.

Remember, you are changing the only lifestyle you know, so change is not going to come easy. You are attempting to undo years of bad spending habits and antiquated ways of thinking about money, so you will surely encounter some resistance along the way.

To say that this journey will come easy would be the furthest thing from the truth. If getting out of debt was easy, everyone would be free of debt.

Change does not come easy. It is a gradual and steady journey, which takes hard work, focus and dedication. When the best climbers in the world attempt to conquer Mount Everest, which is the highest mountain in the world, they break the journey into stages so that their bodies can gradually adjust to the extreme altitude. Without setting up camp and resting for several days, their bodies would not stand a chance as they ascend closer to the peak which is 29,000 feet above sea level. Methodical planning along with inner peace surely play a big role as these climbers attempt this incredible feat.

With a new mindset and attitude change that peace bring forth, you become a different person with a different perspective on life. Your whole focus in life is changed. Purchases that you would not have hesitated on, in the past, are suddenly, not particularly important because you are transitioning away from material things, thanks to the ever-present peace.

Regardless of the amount of debt your trying to free yourself of, it can be a long road filled with many roadblocks and detours. You must trust God and pray for wisdom every day, while on this journey. You must continue to persevere and push forward, even in times of doubt.

17. Two Individuals, Two Repossessions

We have all heard the arguments that are used for justifying the need to purchase a new car. Common excuses we often hear are the need for reliable transportation, not wanting someone else's problems with a used car, a great interest rate or perhaps the deal of a lifetime. Of course, there is also the classic excuse – the new car smell. These are all driving factors that people use to convince themselves and their spouses that a new car is needed. Whatever the case for buying a new car, there is never a good enough deal or a good enough reason if you cannot afford it in the first place. The purchase of a new automobile could cause great financial pain. When you examine a new car from a purely financial standpoint, it is probably one of the worst investments you can make. What other purchase can you make that immediately loses 15% of its value the very day you take it home? On average, vehicles lost between 15-20% yearly.

Mike learned a painful lesson on how purchasing an automobile can hurt you. He learned firsthand how banks react when payments on a vehicle are not made on time. Mike was a little reluctant to share his experience with me because his repossession was very embarrassing and the psychological wounds, he suffered that day are still very fresh in his mind.

According to Mike, getting his car repossessed was one of the most humiliating experiences of his life. Mike vividly recalls the afternoon the repo man backed into his driveway. "It couldn't have happened on a prettier spring day," said Mike.

It seemed as if all his neighbors were out working in their yards, even the neighbors he did not see very often. As a noisy, out of place diesel tow truck slowly made its way down Mike's quiet street, everything seemed to come to a complete standstill.

Mike and his wife made a comfortable living, earning a combined $80,000 annual salary. Both had perceived job security and never really worried about money. Mike's wife handled the bills because he was not good at that sort of thing, so reluctantly, his wife had the title of head bill juggler. That was a title no one wanted, due to the family's tight and deteriorating financial situation.

Mike's monthly $540 truck payment would sometimes go 30 days delinquent, but rarely would it go 60 days. He would get late notices but figured his payment was just arriving at the bank at about the time the notices were received. Mike thought that the bank would figure it out and disregard the late notices sent out. Mike was never notified by the bank that paying this way might be a problem, so he continued to send in the payments this way. Mike always thought that the payment would work itself out. It was not as if they were habitual late payers. Every month was different in the household with some months being tighter than other months. In Mike's eyes, it was "no big deal" because the bank would eventually get their money, plus a late fee, right?

It's a big deal now, because the repo man is in Mike's driveway and all of his neighbors have their eyes focused on Mike's house, halting all yard work on the block.

With the truck note falling on the 25th of the month, it often got left behind and was paid last. With combined credit card debt of $47,000 spread over seven credit cards, it was getting increasingly harder for the math to work to accommodate all the bills each month. Mike and his wife knew they were living too close to the edge, but neither wanted to confront the truth. Debt was an uncomfortable topic, a topic for another day. Plus, they both had secure jobs, so, there was no real reason for immediate concern, at least in their eyes.

Mike's heart began to beat faster and faster as the repo man, came up his driveway with a sled-type truck, where the cars are just pulled up the ramp with a cable and reeled in like a prized fish. Mike recalls not looking up at the neighbors, simply out of embarrassment, as he waited to gather his personal belongings from his vehicle.

Once inside the house, Mike glanced through his blinds to see his truck for the last time, as it slowly ascended the repo sled for the ride to the repo yard. As the truck continued to make its way up the sled, Mike descended into a new low, because of the poor financial decisions made over the years, a low he had never experienced. He immediately sank to his knees and wept out of shame and embarrassment. If there was one thing, he was thankful for, it was that his wife was not home to witness what had just taken place in the driveway for the whole neighborhood to see.

For the first time in his life, Mike was forced to come face to face with his reckless and irresponsible spending. Mike and his wife were living a life larger than their paychecks could support. They were finally forced to face the truth. Unfortunately, it took the repo man, showing up at Mike's house to give him and his wife a wakeup call. It was so loud

that it demanded the attention of the entire neighborhood! That is the punch-in-the-face wakeup call that Mike needed to get his financial life in gear. Their financial rope finally ran out; they had reached the end. That evening, the couple began to come up with a plan to ease their life of the financial strain they had endured for so many years.
Thinking back, Mike recalls that evening feeling like he had gone ten rounds with a heavy weight boxer, when in fact, it only took ten minutes from when the repo man arrived to when he had finished doing what he had come to do.

Monica is someone who also knows firsthand the financial pain that comes with an automobile repossession. I interviewed Monica shortly after speaking with Mike. Monica would get the itch to purchase a newer car once the new car smell evaporated and was gone. Monica worked in cosmetic sales and her position called for a lot of travel, so she felt that a new car was justified every year. She joked that the model of the vehicle should always match the current year.

With every new car purchased, Monica would get the longest financing terms available, which would afford her the smallest monthly payment possible. In most instances, Monica would go for the five-year plans, as she would simply roll each outstanding balance still owed in with the new purchase price. One year, Monica was forced to go with a seven-year plan just to be able to "afford" the monthly payments. With every new purchase, she was paying for the new car along with the remaining balance left on the previous car loan, which were conveniently rolled in and packaged with the new loan.

Monica was engaged in a dangerous game of roulette financing, in which she would eventually lose. You can never win playing roulette auto financing because of the way new cars rapidly depreciate. You are guaranteed to lose every time you play this game. The only winners are the companies doing the financing.

Monica's days of roulette financing are now over as the repo man ultimately caught up with her as well. It was just a matter of time before her rope also ran out as she was unable to keep up with the expensive car payments. Monica's credit is now damaged and reflects a repossessed auto, just like Mike's, which will remain for many years to come.

With the money auto companies spend on new car advertising, it is easy to get caught in the trap of justifying the need for a new car. For many, the allure of a shiny brand-new model, along with the awesome smell, is too hard to walk away from. Throw a savvy car salesman into the mix and before you know it, you are signing up for a five-year trip.

Having secured jobs and regular paychecks gave Mike and Monica a false sense of security. Therefore, in their eyes, there was no real urgency to change the way they were conducting business, because things were manageable, albeit very tight.

Unfortunately for both individuals, it took a tow truck driver to get their attention and to get them to wake up and realize what was going on in their financial lives. Having their automobiles repossessed was a blessing disguised as a wakeup call.

18. EMERGENCY BUFFER FUND

The number one reason people get into debt is because they live ahead of their paycheck and beyond their financial means. They make purchases without considering the long term affects and have no savings to cover emergencies that pop up.

Emergency funds are the difference between staying out of debt and getting into debt. If there is no emergency fund in place, when emergencies come up, big or small, you either must borrow money or use credit cards in order to pay for that emergency. Emergency funds are used as important walls of defense against unexpected events. Without this defense, you are inviting debt to come be a part of your world. An emergency fund is that layer of protection between you and debt. Having no emergency fund is like going to the beach without sun block to protect you against the harmful rays of the sun. The lotion acts as a protective buffer between you and the sun. Without the protection of the sun block, you will pay the price by experiencing some level of pain. Sun block and emergency funds serve the same purpose; both are meant to protect you from pain.

For emergency funds to stand strong, it is important to distinguish the difference between a legitimate emergency and a normal expense. Some people are not sure what classifies as a true emergency. An emergency expense is not a tank of gas, clothes, birthdays, vacations, Christmas gifts or a regularly scheduled oil change. If you drive a car you will need to have your oil changes worked into your budget as part of maintaining the vehicle, so it should not come as a surprise expense. These are predictable and common monthly expenditures that happen often and should not cause panic. If you are not properly budgeting, these occurrences might seem like emergencies.

These expenses must somehow be worked into your monthly budget so that they are never classified as emergencies. Under no circumstances, should you ever dip into your emergency fund to pay for these items or events. Birthdays and anniversaries roll around every year, just like Christmas. Every year we can count on these expenses, whether we are ready or not. True emergency expenses are not as predictable, such as a triple bypass, blown transmissions, HVAC replacements or your house catches fire. These expenses happen more often than you think!

Growing up in New Orleans, we always looked forward to Mardi-Gras with great anticipation every year. Almost two weeks of non-stop parades filled with lots of beads and doubloons. One of the popular parade routes in the city ran along the famous St. Charles Avenue, the street famous for its street cars and historic mansions.
Our family would get to the parade route about four hours before the parade started, to secure a good spot to view the parade. We would pitch our blanket, chairs, and food on the "Neutral Ground" which is the strip of land that separates the traffic running east from the traffic running west. People outside of New Orleans refer to this strip of land as the median. If you remove that buffer, then you remove the protection and the likelihood of more accidents occurring is greater.

Your personal emergency fund performs the same function as does the neutral ground; both are there to serve a purpose and protect. The emergency fund sits between you and every unexpected expense life throws your way. If you remove this fund, you have no protection between you and life, which puts you at greater risk of going into debt. Understanding the difference between a true emergency expense and all other expenses is crucial in building and maintaining a strong emergency fund. The rules must be crystal clear, when tapping into the emergency fund or you will always struggle with debt. The key to staying out of your emergency fund is proper budgeting. Without proper budgeting principles in place, your emergency fund will always be dipped into and will never fulfill its intended purpose.

One way to properly guard against emergencies is by having the right types of auto, disability, life, health, renter's, and homeowner's insurance in place, in the event some big emergency occurs. By having the right coverage, you can minimize your exposure and lessen the financial impact these emergencies could have. These expenses could hit you the hardest if the right insurance is not in place when an unfortunate event unfolds.

All financial experts agree that you must initially have at least $1,000-$2,000 in your emergency fund to handle unexpected events. You need something to go to battle for you when life starts invading with expenses. The $1,000 in your emergency fund will stand up and fight for you just like the sun block fights to protect your body. Eventually, your goal should be to have your emergency fund prepared to handle six to twelve months of living expenses in case of a job loss.

Establishing an emergency fund is not as easy as it sounds, especially if you have never been able to save any money. There is hard work involved in getting your emergency fund established but it is not overly complicated in understanding its purpose when you break it down.

Everyone that has experienced debt at some point in their lives share one common element, no established emergency fund, when unplanned expenses surfaced. Having this fund established is truly the key foundation to having long term financial success. Without this all-important fund in place, you will always be dealing with some form of debt in your life. Having a permanent emergency fund in place is a proven way to stop that vicious cycle of loan and credit card dependency every time an unplanned expense occurs.

19. The Credit Card Balance Transfer Disappearing Act (Becky's Story)

Becky seemed to have mastered the credit card balance transfer act as she had all the right moves at all the right times. With a move here and a move there, poof, she would be able to make a balance on a credit card vanish into thin air or at least give the illusion that it was gone. All this was done without even making a payment!

Becky was not actually making the balance disappear. She was just moving money from one place to another. This was done by simply shifting her balance from one credit card issuer to another, thus making available, additional credit lines so that other transfers could eventually take the place of the balance that was just transferred. She was playing with fire by recklessly transferring these balances, one after another. And it was just a matter of time before she got burned.

In Becky's mind, these financial maneuvers were justified and used as a means of survival. She was doing what she had to do to keep her bills paid and her household sustained after losing her job of fifteen years. Becky had recently been laid off and was receiving unemployment, which barely covered the groceries and her car note. She had no savings and no emergency buffer fund established to protect against unforeseen events like a job layoff. Now the layoff is reality!

These credit card balance transfers were occurring even before Becky had been laid off, even before she was in survival mode, she admitted. She is now in a full-blown survival mode and the fire she is playing with has spread and will soon be out of control.

Becky was managing to somehow juggle seven credit cards with interest rates ranging from 13% to 24%. During this juggling performance, Becky could skip a monthly payment to the credit card companies. This was done by transferring either the entire balance or a portion of the balance from one credit card to another credit card. By transferring the entire balance, no more payments need to be made on that card. The card is paid off. The transfer takes the place of the monthly payment, while also freeing up room for other balances to be transferred in its place.

By moving her credit card balances around, she was accumulating debt at a rapid pace. At this rate she was quickly approaching the point of no return. By only shifting around the balances, no payments were being made on the credit cards, which gave the appearance that everything was fine and up to date. With so many balance transfers occurring, she soon had to implement an accounting system just to keep track of her transfers and available credit.

The longer the period of unemployment lingered, the deeper she was sliding into debt. It was only a matter of time before the credit card companies caught on to all the balance transfers. Once, the credit card companies catch on to what she is doing, they will eventually raise her interest rates and potentially cut her off from further use of the cards. If Becky's credit limits are frozen, things will quickly decline and go from bad to worse with her essential bills quickly falling behind. Becky was using the credit cards as her personal bank account to keep the household bills to pre-layoff status.

With the newly acquired debt, Becky will now have to shift her focus and look for jobs with an income level that will be able to accommodate the new debt.

By searching for jobs with higher income potential, she is limiting the possibility of job openings that might surface with a lower income which might be more appealing and closer to her home.

When a balance transfer takes place, you automatically trigger a balance transfer fee, usually around 3-5% of the amount you wish to transfer (This is what the banks charge for taking on the risk and handling the transfer). For instance, if you are transferring $5000, the fee would be $250, now added to the balance you just transferred. Take for instance a credit card balance of $10,000 at 18% interest. If Becky can only make the minimum payments of 3% each month until the credit card is paid off, she will have paid roughly $19,421 (the original $10,000 plus $9,421.00 in interest) It will take her nearly two decades to pay off the credit card. This is just on one card! Imagine the financial stress Becky is feeling by making only minimum payments on multiple credit cards. She will never get ahead.

By not drastically cutting her household bills and picking up part-time employment, once she learned of the layoff, Becky's financial future is now spiraling out of control, at a rapid pace. Her actions or lack thereof could easily lead to personal bankruptcy or home foreclosure, depending on how long her current situation remains.

By having an emergency buffer fund in place, no credit card debt and by cutting her lifestyle, this job loss would have been manageable instead of a full-blown emergency. Having a couple thousand dollars saved for emergencies would have made this transition period a lot less stressful. Becky would have had the luxury to be able to afford to look for a variety of jobs at different income and stress levels, and not be forced to jump at the first offer out of fear or necessity.

Becky now faces a future with a huge debt load that accumulated at an amazingly fast rate. All of this happened because she did not carefully plan and had no emergency fund to fall back on. She was not the least bit prepared financially to handle anything that could potentially go wrong in her life.

When you lose an income due to a job loss, it can be a stressful time for the whole family, until a new job is landed, and life resumes back to a normal state. That is why it is so important for all individuals and families to have their financial house in order, in case you are faced with some type of emergency, including that of a job loss. The last thing you want for yourself or your family is to have to rely on credit cards to get you through a period of unemployment or any other emergency you are faced with. You certainly do not want to be addressing this lack of planning, while you are in the middle of a job loss. It's like trying to figure out, how a car jack works, when changing a tire for the first time on side the interstate with cars speeding past you at 75 miles per hour.

Losing a job can be a very scary and traumatic experience. The stress of finding a job is great enough, so you do not need added stress of relying on credit cards to provide income.
It is like relying on a cinder block as a life preserver when you are drowning. These innocent looking pieces of plastic have disaster written all over them. Never position yourself or your family to have to rely on credit cards to get through a transition period!

Perhaps we could prepare ourselves better if we all took the approach that our jobs would be ending in six months. This way, we would be forced to examine our own situations and get our finances in order. Start properly preparing your family's finances while times are good, and you are not dealing with some catastrophic emergency. If it takes pretending that you are faced with some big financial event to get you moving, then do it! Do whatever it takes to get your financial house prepared and in shape, so that if you are faced with an emergency, you will be better equipped to handle it.

20. THE COST OF FREEDOM

Is there a price to pay for freedom? That all depends on how bad you want it and what are you willing to sacrifice to get there! For the men who signed the Declaration of Independence in 1776, it meant going to war to stand up for what they believed in. They pledged their lives, fortunes, and sacred honor in order to obtain freedom. Of the 56 signers of the declaration, roughly 1/3 served as militia officers during the war against Great Britain. Not only did these men provide their signatures, but they backed it up by putting their lives on the line because they strongly believed in fighting to gain their country's independence.
At what cost are you willing to pay to take yourself or your family into the foreign land of financial freedom? Are you willing to persevere and do whatever it takes to achieve owing no one?

Fortunately, you do not have to experience the hardships that the signers of the declaration had to endure to reach the goal of becoming free of debt. You do not have to put your life on the line.

The first step in declaring your independence from debt is to start tearing down the life you built up for yourself. Approach it the same way you would if you were tearing down a dilapidated home. Completely strip it down to the foundation, so that you can start over and rebuild it stronger from the ground up.

More and more folks are striping down their lives so that they can rid the debt that exists.

They want more out of life. They have the desire to call their own shots in life and not having their creditors calling them. They desire freedom!

The signers of the declaration were risking everything to gain independence and all you must do is shave your lifestyle.

21. Easing Our Children's Pain (Anne's Story)

All too often as parents, we rush into things quickly when coming to the aid of our children. From the time our children are young, we give them everything to ensure that they have every opportunity to be successful in life. Even as we see them grow and become parents, we still attempt to nurture and help them to the best of our financial ability.

In a valiant attempt to ease her daughter's financial pain, Anne offered to take her daughter's existing credit card debt and roll it into her home mortgage by refinancing. Anne had access to a 45,000-home equity line of credit which is also referred to as a HELOC. This is simply using your homes built up equity as a line of credit. Anne figured that her daughter, Maddy could save a lot of money by paying her back at a reasonable interest rate instead of paying the outrageous 22% percent she was being charged by the credit card companies.

Maddy, a 32-year-old single parent who constantly struggled to make ends meet. Month after month she continued to slide deeper and deeper into debt; relying on Anne to rescue her out of frequent financial binds as she skipped around from job to job.
Anne, a 66 year old retired school bus driver, recently widowed and living on social security. She also supplemented her income by cleaning houses. Anne had been living in her home for the past twenty-two years with eight years remaining on her mortgage. With the new HELOC on the books, along with her regular mortgage, she is now responsible for both loans which are attached to the home.

Anne felt that by removing this financial strain from her daughter's life, Maddy would feel less stressed, find greater peace in her life and focus more on raising her two children. Anne felt that she had a responsibility to help her only child, since she was a single parent with no child support to count on, at least not on a consistent monthly basis. Anne hated to see Maddy struggle and was willing to do anything in her power to help her.

By utilizing the HELOC at a 5.5% interest rate, Anne rolled Maddy's $34,000 credit card debt into her secured line of credit. With the credit card debt now part of the mortgage, Anne's combined house payment was now up to $1,050 a month, and her total monthly income was around $2,350 a month which included her house cleaning income. Under the agreement, Anne was to be paid $250 a month by her daughter until the $34k was paid.

Fast forward two years and you guessed it. The plan didn't go as according to how it was drawn up. Anne's daughter has not paid as agreed due to job instability and Anne hurt her back on a cleaning job and now unable to perform any side jobs which leaves just her social security income. She barely has any money after the mortgage is paid. With absolutely no money left over after the bare necessities were met, Anne was forced to let her signature loans go to collections as she was unable to meet even the minimum monthly payments.

An attempt to help her daughter from a tough financial situation has now backfired on Anne. She has now put her home in jeopardy, not to mention the added stress she now carries, which could threaten her health.

With Anne now in her late 60's, this is certainly not the kind of retirement Anne had envisioned for herself. She was simply not in a good enough financial position to be able to afford even the slightest mortgage increase.

The only thing Anne accomplished by taking out the HELOC was shifting the debt around. The debt simply went from being unsecured to being secured. Anne just picked up the debt and moved it to another place, as if it were piece of furniture. In the process, the financial pain was transferred from Maddy to Anne.

Maddy would have been better off working out payment arrangements with the credit card companies or even settling for a lesser amount on the outstanding debt.

Good intentions, when it comes to money, often have a way of backfiring. What started out as a way for Anne to alleviate pain for a loved one has created more pain and anguish for herself.

Unfortunately for Anne, she is living in a house that she can no longer afford. The house is now a ticking time bomb, just waiting for a possible foreclosure to happen.
Currently her mortgage and HELOC are well over 45% of her monthly income with the removal of her house cleaning earnings. She would be better off finding a home that does not exceed 25% of her monthly income. Anne was eight years away from paying off her house and could almost taste freedom as she was within striking distance of owning her home.

With one hasty financial maneuver, she jeopardized it all. The only way this plan could have possibly been pulled off, (even though it was a little too close for comfort) is if everything went perfectly according to plan; Maddy paying as agreed, no physical injuries, no more credit card debt and no unexpected emergencies. The problem with this plan is that it only worked if everything went exactly according to the script, which, in reality, never happens!

22. Short Selling a Home

Whenever an economic downturn occurs, mortgage terms like underwater, upside down, undervalued, and short sale start to surface and become familiar terms. Simply put these terms are used to describe property that is presently valued at less than what is owed. For instance, if a house is worth $100,000 and you owe $120,000 then it is considered upside down. If a word used to describe your mortgage or your vehicle starts with the letter U, it is usually not a good thing.

We started hearing about underwater mortgages and short sales in 2008 during the sub-prime mortgage crisis. This occurred when home values across the nation started to plummet and adjustable rate mortgages started to adjust and climb. Homeowners with adjustable rate mortgages started seeing their monthly payments skyrocket to the point where they could not pay it anymore. With the rising cost of mortgage payments, families could no longer afford to live in their homes, thus resulting in a spike of short sales and foreclosures across the United States.

With home values sinking, homeowners were not able to pull any equity out of the home, in order to prolong staying there. Homeowners with equity built up can fall back on that equity, in times of need. But with the values falling, this was not possible. Any equity that was in the home had disappeared along with the declining home values.

When buyers purchase a home with nothing down and the value of the property takes a dive, your home is upside down in value. We witnessed this scenario in Ray's story.

Homeowners who come up with a 20% or more down payments at the time of purchase are obviously in better financial positions to ride out declines in property values than those who get into houses with absolutely nothing down. For instance, if you purchase a $100,000 home with nothing down and two years later the home is valued at $80,000, you have negative equity which means you are upside down.

When a home is said to be underwater, and there has not been a recent flood of biblical proportion, it simply means that more is owed on the home than it would sell for.

When a homeowner attempts to short sell a home, he or she is trying to get out of the home by selling it short of what is still contractually owed on the home. If homeowners fall behind on their mortgage and cannot afford to make the monthly payments, they will eventually be served with a foreclosure notice by their lender. The only way around foreclosure is a short sale. Some homeowners are opting to try and short sell their homes in lieu of being foreclosed on.

By doing this, they are entertaining offers below what is currently owed on the loan. The offers they attract will be reflective of the current market values in the area, regardless of the amount still owed on the property. For this sale to go through, the mortgage lender must agree to accept offers, usually below, the amount owed on the home. If the homeowner finds a buyer and the lender agrees to accept the offer, then a short sale has occurred.

Once the short sale is completed, there will likely be a balance remaining on the loan. The deficiency balance is the remaining amount still owed on the loan after the short sale is complete. The original borrower could still be responsible for this amount depending on how the mortgage company classifies the sale.

For instance, if you owe $100,000 on a home mortgage and you short sell it for $80,000, (which is what the houses are selling for at the current time in your area) the lender will be out $20,000.
The lender can now either sue you for the difference or write it off and chalk it up as a loss and not pursue you. In most cases, the lender does not elect to pursue the borrower. For the lender to sue, they must hire expensive lawyers, fill out a ton of paperwork and spend money on court fees in an attempt to recoup their money. The lender understands that the borrower is not in a good financial position after losing the house, so pursuing the borrower does not make sense in many cases.

If the borrower is cornered by the lender, they can always file bankruptcy and make the deficiency balance disappear. So, in many cases the lender elects not to pursue the borrower for the difference. When an offer is made on a short sale, it is always best to try to get the lender to put in writing that they will accept the offer without recourse, meaning they will not pursue you for the balance remaining on the loan after the short sale is complete.

Instead of attempting a short sale, some homeowners are electing to simply walk away and turn in the keys. This practice is becoming known as a strategic default. After assessing their financial situations, homeowners are deciding that it would be a better move financially to take a hit on their credit rather than to stick around in the house and wait to see if the lost equity ever comes back.

Regardless, if a lender pursues the borrower or simply writes off the short fall, the foreclosure or short sale will still reflect on the borrower's credit report. As far as credit bureau reporting goes, there is not much of a distinguishable difference between a foreclosure and a short sale—they will both do damage to your credit score. Credit scores which are also referred to as Fico scores typically drop anywhere from 100-160 points once a foreclosure or a short sale has taken place. A fico score of 680 will drop from 85-105 but a higher fico score of 780 will drop anywhere from 140-160 points. In other words, the higher your score the more it will get smashed. Either way, it will be a while before you become a homeowner again.

23. Keeping up with the Cost of Homeowner's Insurance

When it comes to insurance, you will never find a shortage of words to describe the discontent associated with the cost of homeowner's insurance. Homeowner's insurance is one of those necessary expenses that give us fits year after year, but it is one type of insurance that we would not be caught dead without because for many of us, our home is our biggest asset.

If you have homeowner's insurance, you will notice that nine and a half times out of ten, you experience an increase every year, regardless of what state you live in or if you have ever filed a claim. There is no such thing as a decrease in rates for homeowner's insurance, or any type of insurance for that matter.

With homeowner's insurance showing no signs of reversing its pricing trends in the future, how can homeowners fight back? One way is to shop and compare prices. Shopping and comparing rates are the most effective way to strike back against price increases. By shopping and comparing rates, every couple of years, you can really save a substantial amount of money on homeowner's insurance. In the process of shopping and comparing prices, you will also become a savvy consumer by knowing what different companies charge for providing the same service.

If you have been with the same insurance carrier for three or four years, look back at your initial rate; the rate you signed up with may be vastly different to what you are paying now.

Chances are that your policy has been increasing year after year.

In many states, it is not uncommon to see a double-digit increase in some years, especially with the frequency of natural disasters such as hurricanes, tornadoes, forest fires and flooding. If your homeowner's insurance is increasing by hundreds of dollars each year that can really add up in a hurry.

The problem with homeowner's insurance is that we do not examine it too closely or very often. We do not examine it because we lead busy lives and we also do not fully understand everything in the policy. In most cases, our homeowner's insurance is escrowed in with our mortgage payment, so it is out of sight and easily forgotten. So, by not seeing that recurring bill each month, we tend not to question or get upset with the yearly increases.

The biggest obstacle in changing insurance companies is the time and hassle that go along with making a change. The first step in switching insurance is contacting several prospective companies and listening to sales pitch after sales pitch along with quote after quote. Next, you have the job of deciding which deductible is appropriate and affordable. Once you have selected a new insurance company, you are then flooded with paperwork. Signature after signature, initial after initial, email after email and phone call after phone call can be a very exhausting and frustrating process. No wonder we are not motivated to go through this agony. Once you have been through it, you feel like you need a vacation.

If you make a change and have settled on a new company, you must then begin the process of canceling your current homeowner's policy. This is the process that everybody dreads, because it is uncomfortable for a lot of people, especially if you know or have some type of relationship with someone in that office. Informing them that you are canceling your business and heading to a competitor is difficult for many. Spouses often argue over who will perform this duty.

Worst case scenario is that you might also have to sit down face to face with an agent that will try to convince you to stay put and not cancel your current policy. If the agent is convincing enough, you may leave that office without canceling.

When making an insurance change, throw out all personal feelings and focus only on the financial strength of the company you are considering along with the yearly cost. If you fear that your current company will try to convince you to stay if you show up in person to cancel, conduct most of the communication over the phone or through email.

It is a lot easier to tell someone "no" over the phone than it is face to face. Why do you think so many breakups occur over the phone or via email or text as opposed to in person? Because it is easier, and you face minimal opposition! If you must go into their office to sign release documents, ask them to please have the necessary paperwork ready so you can get in and out quickly.

The longer you are in their office, the greater chance the insurance company has to convince you to stay. However, by going through this hassle and taking the time to switch companies, you will be rewarded in the end.

Let's say that you save $900 annually in premiums by switching your homeowner's insurance. If it takes you a total of three hours to switch your policy from start to finish, you will make a whopping $300 an hour. How many people do you know make $300 an hour? It just takes time, effort, persistence, and a ton of patience to make the switch.

Realizing the potential savings should provide enough motivation to get it done. You how have $900 to pay off a bill or put towards your emergency buffer fund.

When you are looking to cut and save on your bills, homeowner's insurance will usually net you the biggest savings, simply because it is one of your biggest expenses. Reducing this expense will also get you the most excited compared to smaller expenses you cut. Once you realize this savings, you should be motivated and fired up to go further and seek out other bills to save on and possibly eliminate.
A good rule of thumb is that the longer it takes to cut ties with one company and switch to another, the bigger the savings. You can shop and compare rates with the different types of insurance you carry, health, auto, life, and renter's insurance. Let's face it, nobody likes to go through the process of switching companies, but the rewards are great and very satisfying.

24. The Right Kinds of Insurance (Jennifer's Loss)

One sure way to stay ahead of the financial game is to have the right insurance to protect you and your family from major financial disasters. It only takes one major accident or incident to happen without the proper type of insurance in place to sink a family. Whatever catastrophe strikes, the cost will always be substantially lower if the proper insurance is in place. When you purchase insurance, you are basically buying debt protection. It is that simple!

Too often we hear people say, "I can't afford insurance" no statement could be further from the truth. The truth is, it will be more expensive if something happens to you or your property and you are not properly insured. What do you think the costs would be after one week in the hospital without health insurance? How about if you become disabled and cannot work? If you are playing the odds, it would be a safer bet to bite the bullet and pay the monthly premiums to get the right kinds of insurance than to go through life rolling the dice without proper protection.

When it comes to health insurance, would you rather pay a $5000 deductible or $150,000 hospital bill? How about life insurance? What if the person you depend on for some level of support suddenly passed away? With the proper insurance, you walk through life differently. Insurance gives you a sense of peace. It also helps you sleep better.

Life Insurance

Jennifer's life was changed in a second, upon hearing the news that her husband died of a massive and sudden heart attack. With the husband as the only one working outside the home, the family goes from one income to no income. Just like that! The income is lost forever. The family is now devastated with the loss of their leader, husband, father, and breadwinner. Jennifer's husband was 44, non-smoker and no history of heart problems in his family.

Obviously, the news comes as a major shock to the family. Jennifer now has three kids to raise by herself and to make matters worse she has not worked outside the home in eight years. She will now be forced to enter the job market with no specific set of skills.

This situation gets even worse-no life insurance was in place, except for a $10,000 policy, courtesy of her husband's employer. This policy will just about cover funeral expenses. Any remaining expenses will likely have to be put on credit cards, or a loan must be taken out to make up for any shortfall that the funeral might bring.

The couple had talked about getting life insurance but that is about as far as they got. No real steps were ever taken to make life insurance become a reality. Jennifer is now left with a mortgage of $155,000 and roughly $12,000 owed on credit cards.

After the initial shock of her husband's death, Jennifer's attention quickly turned to the family's financial situation. Instead of having the proper time to mourn, she now must focus on survival for herself and the kids. Jennifer knew within minutes of receiving the news of her husband's death, that her days were probably numbered in the house. On that fateful day, a wife lost her husband, lifestyle and possibly the only home the kids have ever known.

This whole situation could have been avoided with a term life insurance policy. With no prior health conditions, being approved for life insurance would have been a simple process for Jennifer's husband. He could have purchased a $500,000 term life policy for ten, twenty or thirty years. For a thirty-year term policy, the price would have been roughly $70 monthly and for a ten-year term policy, it would have been about $30 monthly, which is the cost of two trips to McDonalds. So, for only $30 a month, Jennifer life would have been headed in a different direction.

The problem with death is that it does not advertise when it is approaching. Therefore, we need to be prepared both spiritually and financially. With life insurance in place when a death occurs, the family has the proper time to mourn and the focus can be on family rather than the finances.

Health Insurance

Medical expenses are also a sure way to financially sink a family. Health care prices have always been on a steady rise and will continue. Even with high prices, it is crucial to have some type of health insurance plan, even if it is just catastrophic hospitalization. There are two basic plans on the market, group insurance and individual & family insurance. Those who are covered with individual health insurance are mostly self-employed or whose company simply does not offer health insurance as a benefit.

Health Insurance is a necessity that you do not want to be without in the event of a sickness or an accident. One week in the hospital without health insurance and you are looking at a bill that you might not be able to recover from financially. The leading cause for personal bankruptcy in America is medical bills.

Individual Health Plans

There are several deductibles you can choose from when searching for individual health plans. Most companies offer deductibles ranging from $250 to $15,000.

Your monthly premium will depend on your chosen deductible. The rule of thumb in health insurance, just like other insurance is the higher the deductible, the lower the monthly premium. By choosing a lower deductible, your monthly premiums will be higher.

High deductible plans are better than high hospital costs which could eventually lead to bankruptcy. Some people fear high deductible plans because of the amount of money they would have to come up with if anything were to happen. You should not worry about the "what if" expenses when dealing with health insurance; cross that bridge when or if you ever get there.

You can financially recover from a $5000 health insurance deductible, but you cannot recover from a $150,000 hospital bill.

Health and life insurance needs to be purchased while you are healthy, and things are going good in life. Trying to get health insurance coverage after being diagnosed with an illness can be awfully expensive! A high deductible, low cost plan is better than no health insurance at all.

Co-pay health insurance plans

There is no doubt health insurance can be confusing and tricky to understand. The most common health insurance plans have two parts, the deductible, and the co-insurance. Let's say you choose a $5,000 deductible with 80/20 co-insurance. (The maximum out-of-pocket will be $7500.00-deductible + coinsurance-$2500.00) Once the deductible has been satisfied, you move into the 2nd phase of health insurance, which is called the 80/20 co-insurance portion.

After the $5,000 deductible has been met, you then pay 20% of the medical bills as they roll in, (until you have accumulated $2,500 in your 20% expenses), while the insurance company will pay 80% of the cost. All health insurance plans have an out-of-pocket maximum, which is the most you will pay each year.

Therefore, in a worst-case scenario for a (single) person, the out of pocket expense would be $7,500 in a calendar year. ($5,000 deductible & 20% coinsurance—$2,500 for a total $7,500) If all you do is go to the doctor or get prescriptions filled, then you pay the co-pay without touching your chosen deductible.

If you ever meet your out of pocket maximum ($7,500), your health insurance is covered at 100% through the remainder of the year. So, now's the time to get that rotator cuff surgery that you have been putting off! Once a new calendar year rolls around, you start all over with the deductibles and coinsurance.

These figures will obviously vary with different insurance companies, but they all follow the same basic model. As consumers, we all hope that we can control the costs by just paying the co-pays and not have to go deep into our pockets to satisfy deductibles and co-insurance.

Health Savings Accounts (HSA'S)

HSA's are also extremely popular. They work a little differently from co-pay plans and are sometimes referred to as the "wholesale cost of health insurance," since every dollar spent goes toward the deductible, unlike co-pay visits to the doctor which are not applied to the deductible. On most HSA's, you have a deductible with no co-insurance to deal with. So, it is simple to understand.

All medical procedures are covered at a discounted rate, which is negotiated with the hospitals and doctors. All expenses that you incur will be applied to your deductible. Once you satisfy your deductible, the out-of-pocket expenses have been met for the year. Therefore, your health care costs are covered at 100%, through the remainder of the calendar year.

Once the calendar year is over, your deductible starts all over again, and must be satisfied just like co-pay plans. HSA's also allow you to save money in an IRA-type account, which is tax free. This is in addition to a traditional IRA.

The money you contribute in your HSA account can be withdrawn to cover any qualified medical expense. Most insurers will issue a debit card for your convenience to pay for medical expenses, which makes it easy to track heath care costs. You can only withdraw from the HSA account what you have paid into it.

Renter's Insurance

Renter's insurance can save you a bundle of money if all your belongings are wiped out in a fire or other disasters. Most of all, it is cheap! If you are renting a house or an apartment, calculate all your belongings and put a dollar value on it. Add up the estimated value of your clothes, furniture, electronics, and other miscellaneous items of value. Then take out an insurance policy to cover the cost to replace those items.

If a house or apartment complex catches fire and all your belongings go up in smoke, would you have the money to replace your possessions? Can you restore your quality of life to how it was before the fire? If the answer is no, then

you need to get renter's insurance! For the price you would pay to get a policy, it is a no brainer.
Renter's insurance is a must in today's world. It will cover you in the event of theft, fire, water damage, and lightening, just to name a few. The average price for renter's insurance is roughly $330.00 yearly. This will provide you with around $40,000 worth of coverage.

As renter's you never know who is on the other side of the wall in your apartment complex or what is going through their mind at any given time. Did your neighbor fall asleep with a lit cigarette? Did your neighbor forget to turn off the stove before going to sleep? What about the renter on top of you? Is their tub overflowing? What about burglars? If you do not have renter's insurance, you are relying on your neighbors to behave themselves. Do you really want to put that much trust into strangers?
The only thing separating you from your unpredictable neighbor is a quarter inch piece of sheetrock, which is no problem for a raging fire. Get peace of mind with renter's insurance!

Disability Insurance
Disability insurance is necessary to keep your household going in case of an accident occurring that prevents you from doing your regular job. This policy pays you a specific dollar amount each month, depending on which plan you choose.
These plans usually come with elimination periods of 90 to 180 days. If you choose a plan with an elimination period of 90 days, benefits will start to kick in 90 days after the disability event.

The elimination period is simply the amount of time you must wait before benefits (payments) kick in. The less time you wait for benefits to start, the more expensive the plan.

Your occupation determines your rates. For example, if you are a welder or an offshore rig worker, you would pay more for a policy compared to someone who works behind a desk for a living.

Let's look at auto insurance. When it comes to auto insurance, it is illegal to drive without auto liability insurance. Why is that? Because the insurance is meant to protect the "other" driver in case you are at fault and cause an accident.

So, if you are forced to buy auto insurance to protect someone you do not even know, why wouldn't we buy other types of insurance to protect people you know and love?

Having the right types of insurance protection keeps you in the financial game and above water in this crazy what's-going-to-go-wrong-next world.

25. Identity Theft

If you traveled back to as early as the 1980's and mentioned the term identity theft, not too many people would be able to give you a clear or accurate definition of this term. In the 1990's, as the internet started to take flight and gain popularity, more and more people started to use its convenient features. Companies started to offer their customers the option to purchase their products online and banks even got into the action by offering their customers something called online banking, which came with the ability to check balances, pay bills and transfer funds. The great thing about all this was that you did not ever have to leave your home to pay a bill. Bill paying could now be accomplished without even purchasing a stamp from the post office! With these convenient features also came hidden risks. This new technology attracted and opened the flood gates for computer crafty criminals, and the terms "identity theft" and "hackers" had arrived. With the new technology that the internet provided, criminals could operate from their living room while still in their pajamas. Criminals could attempt to hack into a company's data base and steal an individual's identity without that person even knowing, until after the crime was committed. Companies now spend millions of dollars every year to combat internet fraud to protect their data.

The internet is not only responsible for paving the way for these criminals to launch their careers, but has played a monumental role in turning this crime into an international affair because of how accessible and convenient it is for criminals to engage in this high-tech cybercrime of cat and mouse.

Identify theft is now global and is being fought by every nation on this planet.
With identity theft now quite common and very much a part of our world, the board game monopoly has even revamped its board to include identity theft as a part of the game. Imagine someone bringing up the term's identity theft and computer virus in 1935 when the board game monopoly was being created? Certainly, they would have been laughed out of the room. Boy have the times changed with new technology!

Identity theft occurs when someone gets a hold of your personal information, like your social security number, without your knowledge in order to commit financial fraud. Most of the time, the crime is committed to obtain something of value, like a loan, utilities, or merchandise. The person committing this crime can be someone you do not know, or perhaps someone you do know. As in many cases, parents, guardians, and relatives can easily obtain the social security numbers of family members to obtain something of value.

According to the FTC (Federal Trade Commission) roughly 9 million Americans have their identity stolen every year. The FTC reported that fraud was the top consumer complaint for the first time ever in 2018. Consumers lost nearly 1.5 billion, roughly 40% higher than the prior year.

According to the Javelin report (Consumer Report) women were 26% more likely to be victims of identity fraud than men. The main reason for this is that women are more likely to make in-person purchases at stores and restaurants, where less consumer control exists. Lost or stolen wallets along with credit cards are still the most common avenues for criminals to obtain personal information.

If your personal information is compromised, it is hard to predict how long it will take to clear up the fraud. Many factors may come into play and every situation is different. Did the criminal pass the information to other criminals, and how many accounts were affected? How long had the fraudulent accounts been open before being discovered?

Most crimes are committed within a week of fraudulently obtained personal information. The sooner you detect that you have been a victim, the less the damage will be. Take the steps to correct the inaccurate accounts as soon as possible. The quicker you act, the sooner it will be resolved. Be vigilant and monitor all your accounts closely and look for any suspicious activity on the accounts. Anyone who has been a victim of identity theft can attest to the fact that it is a very time-consuming and frustrating process to clear your name.

Criminals will continue to be on the prowl, waiting for you to mess up. If an opportunity presents itself in the form of a misplaced credit card or other personal information, criminals will seize the opportunity given to them. Criminals do not hold nine-five jobs. They are on the clock 24 hours a day, 7 days a week, looking for opportunities to cash in and spoil your day. When an opportunity comes, they are ready to spring into action. Criminals are always on the clock and only take vacations when someone else is footing the tab. Try not to be the one paying for vacations other than you own.

Always be aware of your surroundings when in public, in order to minimize the risk of being ripped off and identity theft occurring.

It would also be wise to have contact numbers for all your credit cards and bank accounts, along with all three credit bureaus. Most financial institutions offer free apps which can be downloaded on your cell phones for quick contact. If your personal information is compromised, you will be able to get in touch with your bank and credit cards to cancel the accounts and place fraud warnings on them. You certainly do not want to be scrambling for phone numbers if you are a victim. Time is the most crucial element when identity fraud has been discovered. The quicker you stop the bleeding, the closer you are to recapturing your identity and resuming your life.

Steps to take if you're a victim of identity fraud

1) Report it immediately to a law enforcement agency.
2) File a complaint with the Federal Trade Commission. (FTC.GOV)
3) Contact your bank and stay in touch with the same person every time you call, so that the representative is familiar with your situation.
4) Put a fraud alert on your credit bureau.
5) If the fraud involved a credit card, contact the card issuer at once. Some credit cards will limit your liability to $50 and some provide zero liability for unauthorized charges.
6) Get a copy of your credit report and monitor it closely for new accounts that may have been recently opened.
7) If you're contacted by a collection agency on a fraud account, respond immediately and notify them in writing and by phone.
8) Stay organized. Be sure to keep a file documented with all correspondence pertaining to the fraud case. Sometimes it might take a while to get cleared, so you will probably start to accumulate a lot of documents.

9) Take charge and follow up on conversations with credit card representatives. Do not wait for them to call you back. The more effort you put into clearing up this fraud the quicker it will get resolved. Get the name of the representative and try to deal with only one person. By dealing with one person, you eventually establish a rapport, which will make that representative work harder to get your case cleared up.

Steps to take to avoid being a victim of identity fraud

1) Guard your personal information. Keep it locked up in a safe place at home.
2) Do not carry social security cards with you. Memorize your social security number along with your children's numbers. Know what cards are always in your purse or wallet.
3) Invest in a shredder. Shred all documents that contain personal information along with convenience checks that your credit card company might send you through the mail.
4) Do not have your personal checks printed with your driver's license number or your social security number.
5) Do not have your social security number printed on your driver's license.
6) Monitor credit reports. Once a year, request a free copy of your credit report at no charge at (annualcreditreport.com) Credit Karma.com is also a free credit bureau monitoring service.
7) Elect to get online statements instead of mailed statements. This minimizes the risk of criminals invading your mailbox.

8) Be vigilant and alert when paying with your credit cards at department stores and restaurants. Criminals will use their cell phones to capture your information.
9) View credit card statements online regularly to monitor any fishy activity. This is also a good habit to get into to monitor and control spending.
10) Use some form of antivirus or spyware on your computer.
11) Get a post office box to prevent theft from your street mailbox.
12) Never give out personal information over the phone.
13) Shop for credit and debit cards that provide a zero liability on lost, stolen, and unauthorized charges made to merchants over the counter or over the phone.
14) To get extra protection and peace of mind, you can subscribe to identity protection services for a monthly fee. These companies monitor your credit bureau and alert you if any activity takes place and some will even assist you in clearing up any fraudulent activity.

26. Credit Unions

When companies and corporations are being formed, the powers in charge surround themselves with the brightest employees and the most efficient technology available, so that they have the right personnel and tools in place to compete in the open market. If you are just starting to organize your finances, you will want to go out and surround yourself with the strongest companies that will give you and your family the best advantage to succeed financially.

Credit Unions can be a valuable organization that you will want on your side. A credit union is a non-profit cooperative financial institution that is owned and controlled by its members and operated for the purpose of providing personal loans at lower rates, as well as checking and savings accounts and Certificate of Deposit (CDs)

In order to join a credit union, you must first belong to a particular group or organization, live in a particular city, or work for a qualifying business that is affiliated with a credit union.

There are differences that separate banks from credit unions. Credit unions are non-profit organizations whereas banks are for-profit. Credit unions are also owned by their members and banks are often owned by stockholders. Credit unions are operated by mostly volunteer board members, and banks are controlled by compensated board members. Unlike Credit Unions, you don't have to live in any certain area or belong to certain organizations to do business with a bank.

If the need arises and you must take out a loan, using a credit union may be your best option. You will generally find lower interest rates than banks and loan companies offer. It is also easier to qualify for a loan at a credit union than it would be at a bank since their lending standards are more relaxed for its members. Because credit unions are non-profit organizations, they do not have many of the expenses that banks and other lenders have. Therefore, they can pass the savings directly to their members. For years, banks have been trying unsuccessfully to get the tax exemption status lifted that credit unions were granted in 1937 by Congress, so that the two institutions could compete on a level playing field. By having the tax-exempt status, Credit Unions miss out on paying taxes that banks are hit with.

One way that banks and credit unions are alike is that they both offer insurance protection up to $250,000 on individual deposited accounts like checking, savings, and money markets. The FDIC (banks) and the NCUA (credit unions) are both independent federal agencies that serve to protect members who have deposited funds in these institutions. What is not covered by the FDIC or the NCUA are stocks, bonds, and money market mutual funds.

Credit unions are most often used by its members for personal loans and loan consolidations. By paying off and transferring high interest rate loans or credit cards to a low interest rate loan, you can save a ton of money on interest. By doing this, credit union members now have one monthly payment at a lower interest rate. Some credit unions will offer their members Christmas or vacation loans regardless of their credit score if their accounts are in good standing and they have been a member for a certain number of years.

Credit unions exist to provide you with a convenient place to deposit funds and obtain loans at reasonable rates. Best of all, they are non-profit cooperatives, meaning they are not owned by out of state corporations. Credit unions are owned by their members. If you are a member, you own a share of the Credit Union. If you have an opportunity to join a Credit union, take advantage of it. Remember, once you are a member of a Credit union, you are always a member, even if you move outside their qualified area. Keep in mind that Credit Unions will not always beat out banks on car loans and personal loan rates. That is why it is wise to shop around and compare rates when making a major purchase like a home or car.

27. Credit Scoring

Credit scores are commonly referred to as FICO scores. These scores are used by credit grantors to measure one's financial capability, character and capacity. This credit scoring model is used by companies in every industry from insurance firms to employers as part of their due diligence process when evaluating risk. Credit scores gives these companies some insight as to what financial risks some customers might present to their companies if they elect to do business with them.

Credit scores play a huge part in determining what company's charge when loaning money. The FICO score gives creditors a deep peak into your private financial world and exposes all the cracks. Companies can now see how and what you have been spending your money on in the last couple of years and how you have paid back what you borrowed.

This score does not focus on any personal issues, nor does it consider what may or may not have gone right or wrong in your financial life. FICO simply focuses on the math and leaves all personal issues out of the equation.

By applying to companies for credit, you give them permission to get a closer look into your entire financial universe once your credit bureau is accessed.

Your credit score is the difference between a high interest rate and a low interest rate. Your score has the capability to affect every phase of your financial wellbeing. It literally is the difference between paying or saving thousands of dollars of interest over a period.

The name FICO is derived from the Fair Isaac Company that developed the calculated formula that goes into creating your credit bureau score which is used worldwide.

Businesses rely heavily on credit scores when making decisions that could affect their company's bottom line. It is their biggest weapon and their first line of defense in determining whether credit is extended.

Your FICO score does not only play a role when borrowing money. It also plays a big part in determining if you will be able to rent an apartment or a house. It determines if a deposit is required as a safety precaution to lessen the landlord's exposure to possible loss. By viewing your credit, the landlord is trying to gauge how big of a risk or flight factor you could be if credit is extended. Your FICO score condenses pages of your entire financial history into a simple three digit score that tell an apartment manager or any potential creditor everything they need to know about you, so that a calculated decision can be made as to whether or not to extend services. Utility companies will also use FICO scores to see if a security deposit is required before running utilities to a home.

Mortgage companies automatically view your credit, as part of their normal process, if you are applying for a home mortgage or a refinance. Their findings will determine if you will be allowed to live in one of their houses and at what interest rate.

Foreclosures are expensive for mortgage companies. It is vital that they get it right the first time and make sure an applicant is qualified before a mortgage is approved. The last thing mortgage companies want to do is kick a borrower out of the house for failure to pay and deal with the expenses that go along with putting the house back on the market.

Companies that provide services to you also view your FICO score. Auto insurance providers, homeowner insurance companies, life Insurance companies and even your cell phone providers use FICO to some degree. Like it or not, companies place a lot of emphasis on your credit score. They feel this is the most accurate method they have in determining how you will behave with their money, products, or services. These companies have years of data to back up their credit decisions.

When applying for a job, some employers will also want to view your credit history, as a requirement during the application process. Like credit grantors, they also want to know how you have handled your financial business in the last several years. Some companies also demand that you have a certain FICO score in order to be hired.
A potential employer is extremely interested in how you have managed your finances, especially if you are applying for a sensitive position in their company, where money is handled regularly. Employers view excessive amounts of debt as potential liabilities, and fear that if someone is hired with a large amount of debt, they could be more prone to steal from the company, if the situation presented itself.

Banks and Credit unions also rely heavily on your credit score to determine what interest rate (risk rate) you fall into if you are approved for a loan. Your interest rate will determine where you fall on their credit scoring model. The higher the score, the less risk involved in making the loan. The lower the score, the higher the risk in making the loan. You pay according to your assigned risk class. Interest rates and credit scores move in opposite directions. The higher your credit score, the lower your interest rate. The lower your credit score, the higher your interest rate.

FICO scores can range from 300-850, with 300 being the lowest and most costly score to borrow and 850 being the highest score and less expensive to borrow. Each credit bureau will assign you a different credit score based on information it gets from various creditors. Rarely will you have identical FICO scores from the big three credit bureaus.

The three major credit bureaus producing FICO scores are Experian, Equifax, and Trans Union. Your scores with these three will vary, because your creditors are not required to report financial data to all three credit bureaus. One creditor might only report to one or two of the major credit bureaus, thus producing different FICO results.
When applying for credit, most creditors will take all three FICO scores and average them out to get one score, or simply rely on one FICO score, depending on which bureau they subscribe to. Creditors must pay a monthly fee to the credit bureaus to have the right to report financial data to them on a monthly basis. Smaller creditors may elect not to subscribe to all three bureaus simply due to budgeting restraints.

There are five factors that go into calculating your FICO score, with more emphasis on the higher percentages.

1) Payment history - **35%**
2) Total amount of debt owed - **30%**
3) Length of credit history - **15%**
4) New or recent credit obtained - **10%**
5) Types of credit used - **10%**

FICO scores do matter

FICO scores in the mid 700's are generally considered to be very good, while scores in the upper 700's are viewed as excellent. It has become easy to monitor and track your fico score. Some of the big credit card issuers like American Express and Discover will let you view your score free of

charge if you are a customer. Free sites like Credit-Karma.com will also give you a free fico score.
By taking a $100,000 30-year mortgage with a 5% interest rate, you would pay roughly $93,000 in interest, over the life of the loan (without paying the house off early).
If you compare the same amount with an 8% interest rate, you would pay $164,000 in total interest (without paying the house off early). The different in the two loans would be a whopping $71,000 difference.

The huge role that interest rates play in the purchase of a home is undeniable. The higher the amount you borrow, the greater the role interest rates play. FICO scores matter in a big way. They dictate the interest rate you will be charged, which is the difference between additional spending and additional savings. FICO scores will continue to play important roles in home purchases and will ultimately decide whether you are approved for a mortgage.

One way to totally avoid FICO scores along with creditors putting you under the microscope is to save and pay cash for all purchases, thus taking yourself out of the financing game. As long you elect to play the financing game, FICO will be a part of the equation.

By paying cash, you are eliminating some company determining whether you are "worthy" or "good enough" to be a customer. Do not put yourself in a position to have your character questioned or judged by some computer model spitting out a FICO score that may or may not accurately reflect your true circumstances. Make smart purchases with cash and keep your dignity in your corner of the ring. Cash is less complicated and keeps you in complete control.

28. DID I CO-SIGN FOR THAT? (TED'S STORY)

If banks, credit unions and mortgage lenders require co-signers before a loan is granted, there is a rather good reason. They understand statistically, there is close to a 40% chance that the primary borrower is going to default during the length of the loan. According to AARP, when examining student loans, the default rate is higher. Some 49% of private student loan cosigners over the age of 50 end up paying some of that debt. Lenders know this because it is their business to understand how a borrower with a certain credit (FICO) score will react and perform over the course of a loan.
FICO scores act in the same manner a thermometer does when measuring the temperature of a sick child. FICO measures how financially healthy you are when applying to for a loan. After the readings are recorded you are then assigned a score.

By co-signing a loan, you are assuring the banks that you will pay if the primary borrower does not. You are basically guaranteeing the loan. Without a co-signer, the loan in some cases will not take place. That is how much confidence the banks have in their credit rating system. They have years of proven data to back up all their lending decisions. Banks are in business for one reason; to make money. Their bottom line depends on the data and their stockholders demand that loans perform accordingly so that the bank does not take a loss.

As you read Ted's story, you will find that the co-signer, in most cases, is almost always left holding the bill just as the statistics predict with amazing accuracy.

Ted and Julie had been married for three years. Like most young couples, they had dreams of getting into their first home. They had been diligently saving for a deposit to be able to put down on a home. Along with this dream, the couple was also extremely excited about the arrival of their first child.

The couple had a combined yearly income of $53,000. Ted worked in the shipping department for a textile company making approximately $29,000 a year and Julie worked as a receptionist in a dental office, making $24,000 a year.

Returning from work one evening, Ted had received a notice in the mail from a local bank. It was a collection demand letter addressed to Ted, seeking payment of $7,800 on a loan that was taken out years earlier.
The letter was from a bank that Ted recognized but had never done business with. Ted tossed and turned that night with that letter on his mind, unable to get a wink of sleep. Although he did not recollect doing business with the bank, he wondered why the bank would send this notice to him.

He reasoned that banks are smart and do not make mistakes like this because of the potential legal ramifications involved. With his not so common last name, he wondered what the chances could be that the bank would have the wrong person, especially with his last name.

His mind raced in all directions trying to come up with theories about how the bank obtained his name and address. Ted immediately thought that someone had gained access to his identity and taken a loan in his name. Ted had recently read an article about identity fraud and how this crime was on the rise, especially with the internet so widely used around the world. He was certain that this had to be some type of identity fraud and he was a victim.

The next morning, Ted called the 800-phone number listed on the bank letterhead and spoke with a representative, who informed Ted that he had co-signed for a $10,000 loan almost six year ago. Ted was shocked and said there must be some mistake, he had never borrowed that kind of money or even cosigned for that amount.

The representative went on to further explain to Ted that he was a co-signer on a signature loan. Ted listened closely, as the bank employee informed him who the primary borrower had been. Ted just about dropped his coffee as he learned the identity of the primary borrower. The main borrower was a former roommate and friend of Ted's. The two had shared an apartment together for about two years. Ted now recalled that his former roommate had taken out a personal loan to purchase a boat and needed Ted's help. Ted did not recall co-signing anything but did remember signing some document relating to the loan. The bank representative informed Ted that he would mail him a copy of the document with his signature on it.

Ted admitted to the bank representative that when he signed the document, he was not really sure what he was signing. He was embarrassed to admit that he thought by signing the loan document, he was verifying the character and the address of his roommate. Ted figured that his roommate was just using him as a character reference. He did not actually think that he was signing up for a loan. The representative went on to tell Ted that the loan would not have been granted if he would not have guaranteed the loan with his signature.

The bank representative went on to explain further that Ted's roommate had filed Chapter 7 bankruptcy almost two years ago. The bank did not realize that there was a co-signer on the loan until an internal audit revealed the findings. The representative continued saying that the Chapter 7 bankruptcy cleared his former roommate of the remaining amount of $7,800 left on the loan but did not clear Ted from his responsibility as the co-signer. That left Ted as the only one legally responsible for repayment of the loan.

As Ted hung up the phone, his hands were shaking. He had not talked to his former roommate in years and would not even know where to start looking for him. Even if Ted managed to locate him, what would Ted do? What would he say? He had filed bankruptcy and was not legally responsible anymore, even if he did trick Ted into co-signing the loan. Ted realized he was the only one to blame.

Ted wondered how he was going to tell his wife about the $7,800 loan that they would have to start paying on. He also wondered how he could have been so foolish to do such a thing and not even know what he was signing. He now had the embarrassment of sharing this careless act with his wife.

All this time, Ted did not notice the loan on his credit bureau report, because of the bank error in not reporting the loan to the credit bureaus. The bank notified Ted that since they updated their records that this loan would soon be reflected on his personal credit report and was also being sent to a collection agency due to the number of days delinquent.

Ted wondered how this new revelation would affect their plans to purchase a home in the future. The newly acquired $7,800 balance was a huge unexpected blow to Ted and Julie's budget.

With his wife not due to be home for another couple of hours, Ted began to search the internet, so that he could learn more about co-signing. He was shocked to find out that most co-signers end up paying for the loans they guarantee. Ted realized that is what he did. He guaranteed the bank that they would get their money back if his roommate defaulted on the loan.

He next came across what the bible says about co-signing in Proverbs 17:18, "one who lacks sense, gives a pledge and puts up security in the presence of his neighbor."

Ted realized that his "lack of sense" years ago has now come back to haunt his family and their future. Ted understood that this was not the bank's fault nor was it his former roommate's fault. Ted could point the finger at nobody but himself. It was his fault for not understanding what he was signing. He had nobody to put the blame on but himself. Ted had signed up for what is now a cruel life lesson, one that he will hopefully never forget.

With his wife now home, Ted explained everything the bank representative had gone over with him. He explained how his former roommate had filed bankruptcy and now he must pay the money back to the bank. He also explained how this bill had to be dealt with first and would delay their plans to become first time homeowners.

Julie was not as upset with her husband as he was with himself, because she knew this was not intentional. They would have to live and learn by this $7,800 mistake. Plus, she knew that whatever she said was not going to undo what had already taken place.

Julie was quick to suggest that the $4,000 they had saved for the down payment of their future home be immediately applied toward the new debt.

Ted also agreed that he would seek out more overtime and apply that extra money towards the debt. Ted was anxious to get rid of this $7,800 mistake as soon as possible because of the stupidity it represented.

The dream of moving into a new home would have to be put on hold until Ted and Julie conquered this debt. With a new baby on the way, they knew that they would have to live on a strict budget, in order to accomplish their goal of paying off the loan, especially since Julie would not be getting paid during maternity leave.

With the ever tightening of credit, loans will be tougher and tougher to obtain without good credit. Banks and other lending institutions will require people with not-so-stellar credit scores to have co-signers before loans can be granted. If you need a co-signer to qualify you probably should just forget about the loan and explore other avenues, you do not want to pull someone into a potential nightmare scenario.

Ted learned an expensive lesson about co-signing; a lesson that fortunately can be overcome but will not soon be forgotten. When you co-sign for someone, you enter in a contract that will bind you with that person for a long time and could have some unforeseen dire consequences. Relationships between family and friends can be destroyed when you bring finances into an equation. It is wise to avoid co-signing at any cost. Remember, when it comes to co-signing, Just so no!

29. Ray's House of Cards

Once a check has been written and there is no money in the account at the time of deposit to cover the amount of the check, it is labeled an NSF Check. NSF stands for non-sufficient funds. When you write a check, and submit it to a creditor, you are assuring the creditor that sufficient funds are in the account to cover the check.

When a check is written before adequate funds are deposited in an account, you run the risk of bouncing a check and incurring further penalties. Incurring these charges was something that Ray was all too familiar with, as these charges really add up in a hurry.
Since Ray seemed to always be short on money, he made a habit of juggling his monthly expenses this way. To buy some time, Ray would often "float" checks, until he could deposit the necessary funds into his account to cover the checks.

Ray's risky strategy of writing checks before money was in his account was starting to back fire more and more frequently. Companies on the receiving end of these checks will look to recover their funds along with an extra fee for their trouble. Ray was simply writing checks that his income could not back up. He was living beyond his income. After speaking with Ray, it was obvious that these checks were symbolic of a much greater problem, which ultimately would lead to his house of cards crumbling.

Ray was happily married with two kids, ages five and seven. His annual income was $35,000 along with his wife's part-time salary of $8000. Together they had a combined yearly salary of $43,000.

Ray's family was currently renting a 1,300 square foot house, which they were quickly outgrowing. Ray and his wife had rented their entire adult lives and had always dreamed of someday becoming official homeowners.

Ray was constantly reminded by his wife that they should start looking for a home of their own. He was also reminded of their bankruptcy filing five years ago and wondered if anyone would seriously consider him to be "homeownership material" The thought of his bankruptcy never escaped his memory for more than a couple of days at a time. It was as if he wore the bankruptcy stigma around his neck. He was reminded of his bankruptcy on the first of every month, when he would write out the rent check to his landlord instead of writing a check to a traditional mortgage company. Ray felt as if he were throwing his money away by spending it on a rented house that would never be his own. Ray felt at this stage in his life, he should own a house, especially with two kids and a wife. Ray felt as though he was letting his family down by not providing them with a home, they could call their own.

A year earlier, Ray had visited a mortgage broker, at the urging of his co-worker who also had a bankruptcy on his record and was surprisingly approved for a mortgage. To Ray's surprise, the same mortgage broker informed him that even with the bankruptcy on his record and $4,200 current credit card debt, he would quality for a mortgage around $150,000. The best part was that he needed nothing down. Nothing down! Ray was shocked to learn that he needed no down payment, but he did not question the mortgage company; he figured they knew what they were doing. After all, it is their job to know what it takes to get into a home by "identifying qualified candidates." The broker informed Ray that currently no down payments are needed in some situations and that even people who have filed bankruptcy need a roof over their head. He went on to explain that with the large inventory of houses on the market that it is easier than ever to get into a home. If you have been on your job for a couple of years, you will be in good shape, Ray was told. With that meeting, the broker had addressed all of his concerns; the down payment and the bankruptcy, two big hurdles that Ray felt was holding him back from homeownership.

Ray had kept his visit with the mortgage company quiet from his wife. Ray knew that if his wife learned they could possibly qualify for a mortgage; she would continue to push him to go forward with it. Ray was not quite ready for that pressure, so he elected to just keep the meeting to himself.

As a new month rolled in, Ray did what he always did on the first of the month. He dropped off the rent check to his landlord. Ray's landlord lived on his route to work. As Ray got out of his car, his landlord met him halfway down the driveway. As Ray handed over the rent check, she informed Ray that his current monthly rent of $650 would be increasing to a whopping $850 a month. Ray was currently renting on a month-to-month basis, free to vacate at the end of any month if he wished. His landlord now wanted to lock him into a yearly contract along with the new rent increase.

As Ray pulled off in his car, he began to experience a flurry of emotionally charged feelings. He was scared, shocked, and at the same time excited about what had just taken place. He was thinking that this might be the opportunity he was waiting for to become a homeowner. The longer he drove, the more convinced he became that his prayers regarding a house had been answered. He was sure of it! This could not be just a coincidence!

According to the numbers the mortgage broker ran, Ray's monthly payment would be around $850 a month. He remembers thinking that if this is not a clear definitive sign from God, then what is? What are the chances that his rent increases to around the same amount that he could get into his own home? Ray thought it would be silly, to lock himself into a yearly lease for that amount of money, especially when he could get his own place.

Upon arriving at work, Ray was unable to focus as his whole day was consumed with the thought of becoming a homeowner. Ray quickly placed a call to the mortgage broker to see if anything had changed since their last visit. Ray informed the broker that he was ready to take the initial steps to homeownership. The mortgage broker's only question to Ray was if he was still working for the same company to which Ray answered, Yes sir! Ray had decided that when he got home, he would share with his wife everything that he discussed with the mortgage broker, even their first meeting, which was almost a year to the day.

That night, as Ray and his family gathered around the table for supper, he informed his wife of the proposed rent increase and yearly contract that his landlord wanted them to sign. He then went on to tell her about an interesting conversation he had with a mortgage broker a year ago which he had kept a secret until now.

Ray's wife was ecstatic after learning of the news and could hardly finish the rest of her supper. She was eager to jump on the house hunting bandwagon, just as Ray had predicted. That night the couple spent the evening gathering all their financial records the mortgage company would need.

The next two weekends, Ray and his wife went house hunting and quickly narrowed their search down to two houses that they really liked. Both houses were within a mile of the house that they were currently renting. They were also in the $120,000-$150,000 price range that Ray had been pre-approved for. Soon after settling on a home and submitting all the couple's financials, a closing date was set.

The day of the closing had arrived. As Ray walked into the mortgage office, his broker Shawn, along with other mortgage representatives, greeted him and his wife at the door, saying "So, you're ready to pull the trigger?" Ray responded, "Yes I am."

Shawn had all the papers organized that needed a signature. With a few strokes of a pen, Ray, and his wife, at the age of 35, were homeowners for the first time in their lives. It was an exciting and memorable day for the entire family. That evening as the family celebrated at the local steak house, the realization hit Ray as he passed the waiter his credit card that he had not even ran the numbers to see how much money the family would have at the end of the month, once the bills and homeowner's insurance were paid. He quickly convinced himself that if he could make it on his old rent payment then he could make it on his new mortgage payment.

As he drove away from the restaurant, he also remembered that the mortgage broker had not even brought up the $8,300 currently owed on the credit card. Ray thought that perhaps the credit bureaus did not pick it up or that small amount of credit card debt did not really matter. Shawn knew about the bankruptcy but did not mention the outstanding credit card debt.
Ray then wondered why he was even thinking about all this; he was already in the house. He signed on the dotted line was now a homeowner.

The first year in the new home was an exciting time for the whole family. Ray had an extra spring in his step and was the happiest he had been in a long time. They often entertained by barbecuing for family and friends which gave them a chance to show off the house. The entire family also enjoyed taking part in different spruce up projects around the home. It took Ray a little time to get accustomed to being called "official" homeowner. It was a title he was enormously proud to have.

As time went on, Ray felt as though a financial decision had to be made on the house, almost every month. Some were major decisions and some minor, but nevertheless decisions had to be made. The first big crisis came in the form of the central air conditioner which needed immediate attention. After speaking with the AC technician, Ray was talked into replacing the old unit with a newer, more energy efficient one. Putting a band-aid on the old unit and having to call out the air conditioning company every couple of months was getting expensive. Later that month, a tree limb crashed through the dining room window as a severe rainstorm passed through. In the past, Ray could just pick up the phone and call his landlord and the problem was solved, usually on the same day. Now since he is the landlord, there is no one to call for emergencies. He was now the one who had to come up with the money to address the problems. With no emergency fund or savings in place, all repairs had to be put on the credit card. The credit card was the only answer at the time.

Six months later, that same tree that sent a limb crashing through the dining room window now sent a much larger limb to pay a visit to the roof, which caused significant damage. The roof was now free to leak and needed immediate attention. Plywood needed to be replaced, along with shingles. Luckily, no structure beams were compromised by the falling tree limb. The job was too big for Ray to do on his own, so he had to entertain bids from roofing companies. Ray called to get some estimates on the roof and the cost was double, and in some cases triple, what Ray had figured in his mind about $1,500. The final cost to repair the roof was $4,500 and that charge went straight to the credit card. His homeowners deductible was $5000, so it didn't make any sense to file a claim with his insurance company.

With the latest wave of repairs going on the credit card, Ray had quietly begun to question whether he was "home-ownership material." Ray had no idea that as a homeowner, he would have to shell out so much money on repairs. In some months, the car repairs were getting paid before the mortgage and credit cards. Ray wondered how other homeowners manage to do it month after month.

His credit card was now maxed out at $18,400 with late fees becoming a common monthly occurrence. The minimum payment was all he could pay and some months even that could not be paid. Ray's declining credit, along with his debt-to-income ratio, was preventing him from acquiring any new lines of credit. That was the explanation the local banker had given him after he tried to apply for a small signature loan to cover some of the house repairs and to pay the annual property tax.

Ray's house was 30 years old, and for the most part, it was in good shape with some areas beginning to show signs of age. The list of repairs was starting to pile up on Ray. He had to organize them in order of importance, because he did not have the money to address all the repairs at the same time. If it was not car repairs, it was the house. It was always something, and that something always required money to get it resolved. Ray wondered if these expenses would ever stop long enough for him to breathe. With the expenses piling up, the family had no money to do anything. Vacations were not even mentioned. They were literally trapped in their home because the finances were so tight.

Within a two-year period, $9,100 in new charges were put on the credit card. According to Ray, every time they planned on paying the card down, the house needed something or something broke. By this time, the credit card company was calling on a regular basis seeking payment. When Ray had purchased the home, he did so with nothing down and no buffer emergency fund in place. With no down payment on the house there was no equity in the property. He also had initial credit card debt of $8,300, which has now more than doubled. Ray had been falling back on his credit card as if it was an emergency fund.

Each new month ushered in more bad news as things just continued to get worse. Ray's wife was informed that her part-time job was being eliminated due to her company restructuring. This was a major blow, as the part-time salary was the glue that was holding the house somewhat together. Ray was to the point where he was just overwhelmed. He was simply doing the best he could do to juggle the finances. Along with the mortgage payment and the credit card falling behind, there were checks floating all over the place. He had nowhere to hide and nowhere to turn; he was out of ammunition.

The couple had some tough decisions that had to be made. Even with his wife's salary, they had trouble paying all the bills every month. To make matters even worse, Ray was informed that his credit card company was in the process of suing him, which could eventually lead to a garnishment of his salary.

With the possibility of his paycheck being reduced due to a garnishment and the house now two months behind, it was just a matter of time before the mortgage company would come for the house. Ray thought of all his options, including selling the house before the bank took it back.
Ray had a friend in the real estate appraising business and decided to give him a call.
His friend Charles agreed to do an appraisal at no charge just to help Ray out. The appraised value on the home came in at $134,000. Ray had purchased the house for $140,000; the house had dropped in value, as most of the houses in the area had over the past couple of years. Bad news seemed to be in no short supply and kept coming for Ray. Ray's house was officially under water, because he owed more on it than what it would sell for.

That evening as Ray sat quietly in the house while everyone was sleeping, he wondered what happened to his dream. Where did he go wrong? How could he screw this dream up so badly and let it slip away so easily? It had all happened so fast. One day he was the hero getting approved for the mortgage, and now nearly three years later, the bank sees him as the villain and wants the house back. It all happened so quickly, as if everything was a blur.

Ray felt like a complete failure, not only to his children and his wife, but also to his family and friends. His one shot at homeownership ended in disaster. Crash and burn! He reflected on his monthly payment. "It was only $850; how could I not manage that?" Ray now understood that being a homeowner is more than just coming up with the monthly payment. It's all the "other things" that go with homeownership and it was the "other things" that Ray wasn't prepared financially to handle.

It would have been easy for Ray to just sit there and curl up and forget about the last couple of years. What started out as a perceived answer to Ray's prayers, ended up being a total nightmare.

With everything that Ray had been through, his family was still counting on him to provide and take care of them. With the pending foreclosure coming, his family would still need a place to live. Ray had no choice but to get up and fight to find his family a place to live. There was no time for Ray to feel sorry for himself. Life was continuing to move forward, and he had to move with it.

Ironically, on his drive into work the next day, he noticed a For Rent sign on the house that he used to rent. Ray could not believe his eyes; he did not know whether to laugh or cry.

Ray had come full circle. He went from being a renter to becoming a homeowner and back to where he started. As he continued his drive to work, Ray had remembered back to what Shawn, the mortgage broker asked him as he entered his office on the day of the closing.

Shawn asked, "Are you ready to pull the trigger?" Ray had now realized that he was not ready to pull the trigger. He had not properly prepared himself for home ownership while he was renting. He was in no way, shape or form ready to take on the responsibilities of being a homeowner. His house of cards had come tumbling down.

30. What Caused Ray's House to Crumble

Ray's financial situation, was a disaster waiting for the right opportunity to happen. And it did happen, in the form of a mortgage. Ray was in no way financially ready to handle the responsibilities that came with being a homeowner. Ray made the three most common mistakes that people who end up losing their home make; he had no down payment, no emergency buffer fund, and he failed to eliminate all his outstanding debt before becoming a homeowner.

Ray's finances were so tight that all it was going to take was one expected or unexpected expense to pop up and knock him off course. Expenses did pop up as expected and ultimately knocked Ray way off course. Ray seriously underestimated how many curveballs a house can throw at you. But most of these pitches were not curve balls; they were expected and hittable balls. Ray had been a renter his entire life, so he knew how often things break and need repairing. Since he did not have to pay for the repairs, his mind did not register any financial pain associated with the expense.

If you have a $100,000 home, you can expect to pay anywhere from 1%-10% of the home's value just in normal yearly maintenance costs. Under Ray's scenario, he should have planned and expected to pay a minimum of $1,400 for maintenance and upkeep.

Ray's first mistake was purchasing the house with nothing down. By not putting anything down, he did not have any equity in the house and was forced to get private mortgage insurance (PMI), which was another expense he did not anticipate.

By not putting down at least 20% of the value of the home, he was at risk if the property value slipped. As in Ray's case, the value of the home lost $6,000 over a three-year period. He purchased it for $140,000 and three years later, it was valued at $134,000. With the decline in value, Ray's house had negative equity.

If Ray would have saved up for a down payment of 20% ($28,000), he would have had equity, under the same set of circumstances. Other positives for putting down at least 20% is that his monthly payment would have been lower, and he would have eliminated the need to purchase private mortgage insurance (PMI). Also with positive equity, Ray would have been in a much better position to negotiate a sale for the house, if it came down to that.

Another crucial mistake Ray made was not having any money saved in an emergency buffer fund. He had no plan to pay for common household maintenance expenses other than putting them on a credit card. He failed to carefully plan and budget in this department and was not prepared when expected repairs around the house had to be addressed.

Ray also did not do his homework on property tax. This is something that comes up every year that homeowners must pay. It is not an emergency, by any means. Every twelve months, the county sends you a notice of the taxes due on the property. The assessor's office never forgets to send these notices out and they never forget you owe the money. They use this money to fund various public projects around the community along with funding the fire and police departments. Failure to pay property taxes can result in a lien being placed on the property. Every year, property taxes will roll around, just like Christmas. Again, Ray had not properly prepared for this recurring bill. This expense should never be put on a credit card.

Lastly, Ray failed to address the thousands owed on his credit card before he moved into the house. He was behind the eight ball before he even signed for the mortgage. The interest rate on the credit card was eating him alive at nearly 24%. This was the only credit card he qualified for a year after his bankruptcy.

Ray's debt should have been knocked out before stepping foot in that house instead of accumulating debt while he was renting, Ray should have been accumulating savings with the anticipation of purchasing a home in the future.

Moving into a home with debt is like spotting an opposing football team 14 points before you even kickoff. The game has not even started, and you are already down two touch-downs.

Ray should have paid off his credit cards before he even entertained the thought of home ownership. Not only did he not pay down the debt, but he incurred new debt on top of the existing debt, with the purchases of new items and repairs to the home. By charging those items for the home, he was limiting his future. No piece of furniture should be that important to take away your freedom. Ray should have focused all his energy into eliminating the existing credit card debt and building up his buffer emergency fund, even if it meant taking on a second job or working overtime.

Ray jumped into the house quickly with both feet. He jumped in and did not know how to swim around the obstacles he faced on a monthly basis, because he did not prepare himself properly. He figured that if the house payment was close to the rent payment, then it would be a no brainer.

Again, he was not looking past the mortgage payment. His vision was stuck on the rent payment and failed to see the whole picture. Ray viewed his rent payments as wasted money, instead of viewing it as an opportunity to get his financial life in order. When the opportunity finally came for Ray, he failed to implement any form of a budget, once inside the home. Without a budget, he did not know where his money was going. He did not even know how much money would be left over after all the bills were paid.

He also failed to ask the "what if" questions that every homeowner needs to ask before moving into a home. What if my wife gets laid off? What if I get laid off? What if the air conditioner goes out? What if the car needs new tires? How much is my homeowner's insurance deductible? How much of an increase in my electric bill can I expect in the middle of summer? You ask these questions, before you go to the mortgage closing, not when you are already in the house.

When Ray's landlord notified him that the rent would be going up, he reacted in a hastily manner, thinking this was his time. And it could have been, if he had started planning earlier.

Ray was correct, when he said he could afford the monthly payment. But that was all he could afford. He could not afford anything beyond the monthly payment. Ray will now have to live with the stigma of having not only a bankruptcy on his record but also a foreclosure. Having gone through the bankruptcy, Ray should have emerged from it with a willingness to never again be associated with any form of debt. After the bankruptcy, Ray resumed living his old lifestyle; the same lifestyle that was responsible for landing him in the debt that led to the bankruptcy.

The spending decisions we make today will always have to be addressed at some point. Ray is now crystal clear on that. He also knows it will be a while before he qualifies for another mortgage. Hopefully, next time, he will be much wiser and better prepared.

The experience of owning a home for the first time should be and can be an enjoyable time in one's life. It can be if proper planning is done. If not, it can be a nightmare that robs you of your sanity and peace, as Ray and his family experienced firsthand. Ray and his family did not own this home; the home owned and controlled them.

31. HELD HOSTAGE BY OUR OWN HOMES

More and more Americans are stepping into mortgages they simply cannot afford. They are purchasing houses they "qualify" for, instead of purchasing houses they can actually "afford." There is a big difference between qualifying and affording. The difference is usually foreclosure. Families who are in this situation find themselves with-out much money left over at the end of the month once the mortgage payment and the other bills are paid. With nothing left over, homeowners are forced to shut down and stop living. Their whole life changes and shifts direction. They must decline invitations to birthday parties and social events. Also gone is eating at restaurants and attending sporting events. Some even stay away from church, to avoid the embarrassment of not being able to give when the offering basket is passed around. Others don't even answer the front door when the girl scouts come around selling cookies. By staying shut in their homes, they can avoid the embarrassment of admitting that they are over extended.

They are literally held hostage in their own homes, because of the mortgage traps they have managed to step in. Some are living in homes they were not able to afford the day they moved in. Their homes are literally sucking close to 40-60% of their monthly income, when no more than 25% of their income should be dedicated to the mortgage. Credit cards, fixed expenses and other loans are laying claim to the remainder of their income. Some would prefer to keep on struggling with the house payments in order to avoid the embarrassment of having to admit to family and friends that they purchased too much house and must now down-grade and find a house they can afford. They feel as if life is passing them by and all they can do is watch from their kitchen window as the rest of the world goes forward. In this material world we live in, the word up-grade has come to symbolize success and down-grade has been viewed as failure.

These folks are all guilty of over purchasing when shopping for houses. They picked the biggest and fanciest one on the block and ignored the most affordable ones—the ones that would allow them a chance to breathe. They chose to impress! They failed to plan for a life once inside the house. Whatever they qualified for, that's what they got. If they qualified for a $250,000 home, then that's what they got. When you over purchase a house, you are trading your freedom for the house. Life's too precious and short to be making that kind of a trade.

When you're in this situation it's easy to give up and lose hope. You feel as if a sign sits in your front yard that reads "debtor's prison." "We purchased more house than we could afford and now we're stuck inside, unable to participate in life," say many new homeowners.

In the majority of cases where the mortgage payment is out of control, the house is not the sole culprit for the financial mess. It's the debt that is brought into the house or accumulated after moving in, which makes it appear like the house is the villain.

If the credit cards and other debt are taken out of the equation, the affordability of the house would not be that big an issue. By having a house payment that is taking up 40-60% of the income, it could be manageable for a period of time, if absolutely no other debt existed. It's guaranteed to be a rocky road with such a high percentage of the income going to the mortgage, which is bound to bring some sleepless nights.

So, if you find yourself in this situation, how do you escape from a home that is holding you prisoner? In order to free yourself and regain your life, you must devise an escape plan in order to break loose from the debt. You must decide if you want to keep the house or sell it! All financial escape plans include restructuring the finances in order to free up some cash. If you want to get back into life and start participating, you will have to either increase your income or start cutting expenses, in order to lower your monthly bills, so that you can create some room to move around. This room to move around is called financial margin and you don't want to be caught without it!

If you decide to stick it out and stay in the home, then you need to start establishing some margin by eliminating debt. By over purchasing a home, you automatically eliminate any chance to build and sustain margin. Without any margin in your life, you will never gain any financial ground.

By having an emergency buffer fund, you are establishing margin. By having margin, you can break the destructive cycle that keeps sending you to lenders and landing you in debt. An emergency fund takes the place of credit cards and provides you with some security in your life. The cool thing about having an emergency buffer fund in your life is that it doesn't charge you interest if you must use it because it's your money.

Financial margin is what is between you and a mountain of stress patiently waiting for an opportunity to pounce on you. The wider the degree of margin, the lesser the stress will be. The narrower the degree of margin the greater the stress will be.

People who are in debt share one common denominator. They have no financial margin present in their life. And when life smacked them, nothing was there to protect them and absorb the hit. Every qualified financial planner will tell you, the key to staying out of debt is to have financial margin.

If you find yourself shackled with an expensive home, car, boat or out of control debt, there is always a way to free yourself. You start by asking yourself straightforward questions. By getting rid of what major expense will provide the greatest financial relief? You then focus all your time and energy exploring ways to accomplish that goal.

By making room and clearing out burdening bills from your life, you allow yourself to financially breathe. By knocking down debt in your life, you will be able to escape the walls in your home that seem to get closer and closer when you're held hostage, in your home. By having room in your budget to financially stretch, you won't have to decline birthday invitations or family events anymore. You are free to leave your house and participate in life.

32. Bankruptcy

Bankruptcy is a gut-wrenching dilemma that many individuals and families are faced with each year. After exploring all options, some have no choice but to file for bankruptcy protection, while others are looking for a quicker way to remove debt and get on with their lives. Some bankruptcy filings offer discounted payment plans and other filings allow you to just walk away from the debt after liquidating certain assets to pay creditors. Whichever bankruptcy you choose, it will always be a part of your life even after it falls off your credit report. Bankruptcy manages to resurface in conversations, employments applications and renewals of various professional licenses. It never completely leaves, even after being officially discharged in bankruptcy court. The stigma of being in that ominous club remains with you long after the bankruptcy has taken its course. The two most widely used forms of bankruptcy are Chapter 7 and Chapter 13.

Chapter 7 Bankruptcy

This form of bankruptcy is also known as "total liquidation," meaning all assets are "liquidated" to pay creditors. This is a proceeding under the Federal bankruptcy law whereby an individual or a company's assets are turned over to a bankruptcy trustee to pay off incurred debts, thus freeing the individual or company from all liability. There are no payment plans set up for chapter 7 bankruptcy. It is fast and to the point. Once the assets are liquidated, you are discharged from the debt without any legal responsibility to pay further. For an individual, this can remain on your credit report for 10 years.

Chapter 13 bankruptcy

This form of bankruptcy is referred to as a "Re-organization," meaning the debts are simply re-organized so that a percentage of what is owed is repaid to certain secured creditors.

Chapter 13 bankruptcy permits you to work out a payment plan for your creditors, overseen and enforced by the bankruptcy court. The payment plans usually run between 3-5 years. Most unsecured lenders will not get paid, some will only get a percentage of their money back. A Chapter 13 bankruptcy remains on an individual's credit report for 7 years.

In 2005 the United States Congress passed the Bankruptcy Reform and Consumer Protection Act. This act makes it more difficult for individuals to shed debt by declaring bankruptcy. This law established a means test in which you must document your income and expenses to see if you qualify to file chapter 7 (total liquidation) Bankruptcy. Your total income for the last six months must be less than the medium income for your state to qualify for a chapter 7 bankruptcies.

If your income is greater than the medium income in your state, you must take further tests that will consider your outstanding debts to see if you still qualify to file a chapter 7 Bankruptcy.

If you fail the means test, the only bankruptcy you may be eligible to file will be a Chapter 13 re-organization, which will put you on a three to five-year payment plan.

One option available to avoiding a Chapter 13 bankruptcy is to contact your creditors individually to work out payment arrangements. When contacting your creditors, it is important to let them know how dire your financial situation has become, and that you're exploring options in lieu of filing bankruptcy.

By working out payment arrangements with your creditors, you can literally do on your own what a Chapter 13 bankruptcy does but without having the stigma of bankruptcy for the rest of your life. Your creditors will probably be more amenable to negotiate a settlement then to see you file bankruptcy. If the bankruptcy court can get you on a payment plan, why can't you get yourself on one?

Families and individuals that are contemplating bankruptcy should examine every angle thoroughly to see if bankruptcy is the best option available to them. In some cases, bankruptcy cannot be avoided and is probably the best option. In other cases, bankruptcy can be avoided by realigning finances and making tough sacrifices. When trying to decide the best route for you or your family, keep in mind that some debts can't be included in a bankruptcy, such as student loans, tax liens, alimony, child support and loans obtained illegally through fraud.

But remember, even in the worst-case scenario, there is life after bankruptcy. Time can certainly lessen the emotional and credit scars that can be left in the wake of a bankruptcy.

33. Understanding Collection Agencies

We have all heard the line, "Life is like a box of chocolates-you never know what you're going to get," made famous by Tom Hanks in the hit movie *Forrest Gump.*

The same can be said for collection agencies-you never know what type of agency you will be dealing with if you are placed for collections by one of your creditors. Dealing with collection agencies can certainly be a mixed bag of surprises. There are a lot of professional agencies out there, unfortunately they get grouped together with the unscrupulous ones. The only time collection agencies make the headlines is when the unscrupulous ones cross the line by breaking the law.

Some unprofessional agencies are known for their aggressive collection styles and abusive tactics when attempting to collect a past due debt. Collectors only get paid if they get someone to pay. That is why they are so aggressive.

It is no secret that most of these agencies employ a percentage of convicted felons and swindlers in their call centers. The lure of the quick buck, minimal experience, and the need to fills chairs by the employers is what draws many to this field.

Most felons are slick talkers and conmen by nature. The bullying aspect of this industry is quite appealing to them and is right up their alley. These exploitative collection companies usually come and go quickly. They are either sued or put out of business by their State's Attorney General's office for violating laws. After being shut down, they usually resurface under a different company name in a different state. Since they are corrupt in nature, it is just a matter of time before they are exposed and shut down again. This cycle continues to repeat itself as long as the opportunity exists to make a quick dollar. With the way people continue to overspend and live beyond their means there will always be a market for these agencies.

All collection agencies must adhere to the Fair Debt Collection Practices Act (FDCPA). This is a set of laws that are meant to protect the consumer against abusive debt collectors. The problem is, not all agencies follow these laws. If you are a victim of one of these abusive agencies, you have rights. You can report them to your state Attorney General's office along with the FTC (Federal Trade Commission).

Collection agencies have two business models by which they operate. They either work for a client who owns the bad debt, or they have purchased the bad debt for pennies on the dollar and now own it outright. Either way, they must collect on the debt to make money.

Most collection agencies work on a contingency basis; meaning, they only get paid when they collect on the debt. Agencies work for a variety of clients and will keep anywhere from 20-50% of the amount of money collected. The clients that agencies work for have written the debt off their books so anything that is paid back is earnings that were not expected.

Some agencies own the debt they are trying to collect on. They have purchased the loans or credit cards from banking institutions. These agencies tend to be more aggressive in collecting "their own" money by suing or resorting to more aggressive tactics to recoup the money they have spent on the debt.

Most agencies and law firms will attempt to collect on the debt but will be quick to sue and obtain judgments in courts of law against the debtors. A large percentage of debtors that have been sued do not even show up for their court date. The collection agency that has brought the suit forward is awarded a judgment in default by the Judge, since the debtor did not show up to contest the alleged debt.

If you are served papers over an alleged debt and feel the debt is not accurate or you do not owe the money, by simply showing up in court, you are almost guaranteed to have the case dropped. When debt is sold from company to company, paperwork is often lost and not accurately passed down in some cases, so the chance of an error occurring is great. Plus, these companies that bring the suits forward are not interested in suing anybody that is going to put up a fight. They keep their fingers crossed and hope nobody shows up in court.

The collection companies that purchase debt in bulk from major banks also file lawsuits in bulk, which tie up the court system. Judges are seeing more and more civil suits filed every year and must limit how many of these suits they will hear each month.

If you have a debt that has been placed for collections, you have a great chance of getting a deal on what you legally owe. You do not have to wait until the Friday after Thanksgiving to get a deal. Black Friday occurs every week in the collection agency world. Every Collection agency is willing to work out some type of deal, whether it is a settlement or payment arrangements.

Agencies are anxious to get paid and close files. The longer the debt stays around, the more money they lose and the less collectible the debt becomes. So, the agencies are willing to negotiate so they can get paid.

Settlements can usually be negotiated anywhere from 40%-60% off the original balance that was placed for collections. If you do settle for less than what is owed on the debt, get ready to receive a 1099-C form. Most creditors will go through the trouble of filling out these forms; some simply will not bother.

A 1099-C form is sent to you and to the IRS by the original creditor, when more than $600 of debt has been forgiven. You must pay taxes on the forgiven amount at your personal income tax rate. The IRS categorizes this as income. Many people mistakenly think that when a debt is charged off by a creditor that it has been canceled and nothing is owed anymore. This is not true. You still owe the money. The creditor simply charged the account off the company's books to show it as a loss.

When dealing with agencies, you have two options. Settle the account in one lump sum or set up payment arrangements. More payment arrangements are entered into with collection agencies than settlements, simply because most debtors do not have the financial resources to come up with the money to pay a lump sum settlement.

If you do enter in settlement arrangement with an agency, make sure you get the settlement documented and in writing. Make sure the settlement agreement is on the collection agency company letterhead. You also want to make sure you keep the letter from the agency outlining the details of the agreed upon settlement, so that years later you are not contacted by another agency pursuing the same debt.

Once you have agreed on a settlement amount, send the agency a certified check. A certified check is recommended so that the agency will not have the information from your personal account. The last thing you want is for your personal checking information to end up in the hands of an unscrupulous collection agency.

The same steps apply if you enter into payment arrangements with an agency. Send the collection agency certified checks to minimize the risk of fraud. Sure, it is a hassle to go through the trouble of getting certified checks. It will be an even bigger hassle if your checking information is compromised and your account is cleaned out by the agency.
It is understandable why people avoid collection agencies, especially with the reputation they have managed to manufacture over the years. Your problems will not disappear by avoiding agencies. Deal with them, negotiate with them, and face them head on. The sooner you start negotiating with them, the sooner you get them out of your life.

When contacting an agency, try to deal with one person. Get the representative's name the first time you call so the representative will be familiar with your situation. If you feel that you are not being treated professionally, ask to deal with another representative or simply communicate only in writing. Do not be intimidated by collection agencies; research and know your rights. Knowledge is power.

Take charge and start working to get collection agencies out of your life. Get busy, come up with a plan and get it done. You got yourself into this mess, now work to get yourself out. Remember, the collection agencies want the debt gone just as bad as you do.

Debt consolidation companies
If you watch television, chances are you have seen commercials advertising debt consolidation companies. These

companies advertise at every hour of the day and basically promise to settle a percentage of your past due debt, for a fee. If you owe $10,000 on a credit card, they will attempt to negotiate a 50% settlement with your creditors. Therefore, you get out of paying $5,000. They intervene on your behalf and deal with the collection agencies, thus taking you out of the loop.

Debt consolidation companies charge thousands of dollars, due upfront, to perform this duty on your behalf. The greater the amount to settle, the more they charge. This money does not go towards your debt. It goes directly into the pockets of the debt settlement companies. This is how they make their money. They always get paid before your creditors.

The debt consolidation companies will give you one set of instructions once you sign up with them. "Ignore your creditors, don't pay them, and refer all calls and correspondence to us!"
By ignoring your creditors, your debt falls further behind and your creditors are more willing to listen to settlement offers. Your credit rating is also in a free fall, while you are ignoring your creditors.

Debt is like an avocado, the longer it sits, the softer it becomes, the easier it is to eat. The same principle applies to your debt. The longer it sits, the softer it becomes, so the easier it is to settle.

You do not need debt settlement companies to take care of your debt. You can negotiate directly with collection agencies or creditors. You can do the same thing the debt consolidation companies do and save thousands of dollars by cutting them out of the picture. Consolidation companies simply act as the middleman. By eliminating these companies, you can apply more money to your outstanding debt and be out of debt quicker.

Remember, once you settle anything over $600, you will trigger a 1099-C (debt cancellation) that will be sent out to you and the IRS. Get ready to pay taxes on the amount forgiven at your personal income tax rate.

34. Uncovering Your Purpose in Life

At some point, in our lives we have all asked the question, why are we here on this earth? This question certainly comes up, if we are burdened by debt, addiction of some kind or the loss of a loved one. We often hear the phrase "there is a reason for everything" or "everything happens for a reason" Have you ever asked yourself, why did you "happen" on this earth? What is your "purpose" in life? Is there a grand plan for our short lives? It is easy to ask these questions when our lives are off track and we are confused as to which direction we should be heading. Ironically, these questions only seem to surface when things are not going as planned in our lives. These questions never pop up in our minds when things are going well. Why is that? Is it because, when things are going well, we feel as if we have direction and know what our purpose on this earth is? As opposed to not knowing what our purpose is, when things are not going as good. Do we have to feel good, in order to have purpose in our lives?

When it comes to serious debt in our lives, we constantly question our purpose. Is it because of the slavery type environment that our debt puts us in or is it because of the stress we feel?

Debt and stress go hand in hand. The stress is simply a by-product of the debt. It comes free of charge and you cannot sign up for debt without the stress attached to it. It is a packaged deal.

Debt certainly has a way of magnifying our problems and questioning our future, or lack thereof.

When the question is asked, "what's wrong with my life," the first thing we blame our debt struggles on is our job. If we are married, the spouse is next in line to take the blame. Someone or something must take the blame for this misfortune! We tend to feel that if only we would have a greater income and have a better job, all our problems would be solved, and life would improve.

Why is it that most people think the answer to all their problems in life is their job? Is it because money manages to play such a big role in our perceived happiness? Would more income solve our problems and make us happier by making more purchases? Have we really been dealt such a bad hand when it comes to our jobs? Or do our financial problems just blow everything out of proportion to where it appears that way? Marriages also share the blame for a life gone wrong. Would we really be better off with someone else, instead of trying to repair the current marriage? If we move to another spouse, aren't we still carrying our troubled luggage into that marriage? How would the marriage be if we focused on fixing some of the problems? These are all questions that we ask, when we are lost and in pain, and struggling for direction in our lives. Somehow or another, we have lost hope and we stop shooting for goals. Without hope, determination and a plan, there can be no future.

So, how does one get out of a dead-end situation? You start by isolating and zeroing in on the parasites that are causing you all this pain. You cannot begin to formulate a comeback plan, until you have properly identified what or who is causing you the misery you are facing. You first must know where to look, in order to find the root of the pain, so that you can attack it and find a way to resolve it. Believe me, when you are hurting, it is not hard to locate the source of the pain!

Start by examining the major players in your life, like your girlfriend/boyfriend, job, boss, spending habits, spouse, house, expensive automobiles, booze, drugs to name a few. If some of these major players are causing you pain or grief, look and pray for ways to fix these problems that are causing you the greatest pain. By attacking the greatest pain, you will feel the greatest relief. After you have examined and come up with a plan to deal with all the major pain producers in your life, focus on what is missing from your life. Your pain could possibly be coming from something that is not currently part of your life. It could be, for example a meaningful relationship that you long for, a broken relationship with a sibling, friend, son, daughter, or a parent. Perhaps, your pain could be coming from a missing relationship with Christ. If you have caused any of these relationships to sour, be humble; learn to forgive and to ask for forgiveness. If you were not the cause of the problem, swallow your pride, extend a hand to try and bridge the distance. Life is too short to let any unsettled issues or pride get in the way of reconciling a broken relationship. By pinpointing the direct cause of the pain in your life, you can begin to get help and turn the tables on your problems. There is a solution to every problem that exists. It is up to us to find the proper solution to our problems.

Take for example, debt. If this is the cause of your pain, imagine for a second if you could magically remove all debt from your life? If you could eliminate any major problem causing you pain in your life, what would your life be like? Would you still feel like you have been dealt a bad hand? Every problem can be compartmentalized and dealt with separately.

If debt is the root of your problem, work to eliminate it, so that it does not continue to affect another part of your life. If you eliminate one issue that is causing you pain, you can indirectly help to correct another issue related to it. For instance, high levels of debt might make it easier for verbal confrontations to occur in the home, between a husband and wife. By working to eliminate the debt, you automatically improve your life and your marriage. The verbal confrontations are a by-product of the lingering debt. The sooner you address and start to tackle any problem at its core, the closer you are to discovering a purpose driven life.

When things are bad and out of control in our lives, we tend to focus on our whole life and say it's all bad. We tend to think there are no bright spots in our life, when in fact, you could throw a dart in any direction and hit a bright spot. It is not all bad, it only appears that way, when you are down and depressed. There are bright spots in everybody's life. Certain aspects in your life are making you feel hopeless and need addressing. Break down and dissect your life into pieces, look at what is specifically causing you pain and restlessness. Whatever the problem is, you must be willing to take that first crucial step, which is always the hardest. Admit there is a problem and seek help. Work to eradicate the biggest problem to the smallest. You will begin to see a drastic improvement in your life.

With only one bad apple in the bunch, you do not write off all the other apples. Remove the rotten one from the bunch and the rest will start to improve by default. If a disgruntled employee threatens to infect all the other employees with words or actions, then management must remove that one employee, before some form of cancer spreads throughout the entire company. A football player with a rotten attitude can negatively affect and influence the entire locker room. That player must be removed, so that the team can remain focused without distractions. Just as a football coach does not replace the whole team because of one losing season, he will pinpoint certain players that are not performing at the level they are capable of and replace them.

It is easy to see, why we question our own existence and purpose with the countless number of problems that can surface in this world. Whether it is debt or any type of addition, we are unable to focus on our God given strengths, if our lives are continuously cluttered with junk. Our minds will not allow our thoughts to wander past the mess we have created. We are trapped, in every form imaginable; prisoners in our own minds with our thoughts even held captive.

Existing just to pay on debt or sustain a bad habit is not living. This is not what God had intended for our lives. You did not just "happen" on this earth so that you could pay bills or support bad habits, your entire life. You cannot realize your full potential unless you pull yourself out from the pile of whatever you have accumulated. Everyone is uniquely gifted, and it is our duty to uncover our gifts and apply them to our families and communities.

Our gifts will never be uncovered and realized, if we allow debt or any other type of vice to dictate and rule our lives. We must continue to strive for a more rewarding life, especially during uncertain times. We owe it to ourselves, our families to break the cycle of debt or any addition that is dragging us down. There is no mountain of debt or addiction that cannot be overcome. If you have a thirst and search hard enough, there is always a solution to any problem.

Once you decide that you're sick and tired of being sick and tired, the spring in your step will begin to come back. You no longer drag yourself out of bed. You now bounce out of bed. Soft words replace harsh words, when communicating with a spouse other family member. By taking positive steps, there can be a new sense of peace and confidence in your life. Your ears will begin to open, and you will be able to hear things that you have not heard in a while. The simple and free things in life are suddenly clear and exciting. We can now hear the chirping birds, the trees dancing in the wind. There is a quiet "still" now present in your life.

It was once said that the mind is like a parachute, unable to work unless it is open. Having taken steps, to rid your life of whatever was holding you down, your mind is now free and open for business.

Once you emerged from whatever bondage, had kept you out of life, a brand new exciting world is open and awaits you. With a new outlook on life, a new attitude along with a new meaning will emerge. You will be able to do things with your family and friends that in the past, was not possible, because of the bondage you were experiencing. Along with a new attitude comes a new confidence, which will make you a stronger person and allow you to do more rewarding things in life.

There is a reason and a purpose for everyone and everything on this earth. It is our job to find out why we were placed on this earth and what we are supposed to do with the short amount of time we have left on earth. What is our mission in life? What is our purpose here? Sometimes these answers come early in life. Sometimes, it takes a lifetime of journeys filled with mistakes, bruises, and important lessons to finally figure it all out. If we are not sure of what our purpose is in life, we must continue to be vigilante as we search and pray until we find the answers.

35. Avoiding Peer Pressure (Arnold & Cindy's dilemma)

Whether you're a corporation, sports team, individual or a family, if you're seeking certain results, these results will not be realized, if there is not a solid plan in place to achieve them. Every leader will tell you that planning is essential for anything that you are trying to successfully accomplish. Without a solid plan, there can be no realistic goals since there is no clear direction or path on how to get where you want to be. When a plan is drawn up, all the different variables are examined, including the things that are supposed to go right, along with the things that could go wrong. This is done so that the "surprises" along the way can be dealt with and overcome.

When a demolition company is called in to implode a high-rise building, careful planning is a must, in order to prevent injury to bystanders and demolition workers. Preventive steps also must be taken to avoid damage to other close-by structures during the blast. The demolition company will start their planning months in advance of the scheduled implosion. During the planning stages, all the wiring and the dynamite are mapped out precisely to ensure that every piece of steel and concrete falls exactly where it is supposed to fall. It is crucial that every piece falls exactly how it was mapped to fall. If one section falls incorrectly during the blast, it will influence how the rest of the building drops. Once the wiring and dynamite are in place, the demolition company will review it again and again, to make sure nothing was missed the first time. Then meetings are held to make sure every piece of dynamite was strategically placed and to rehearse what everyone is supposed to be doing before, during and after the blast. All demolition companies know that the key to reaching their goals is a ton of preparation along with careful and methodical planning. There is no room for even the slightest error to occur. They must get it right the first time, because lives, profits, and reputations are on the line. There is not a second chance to do it right when imploding a building. Once it is down it is done.

Planning along with the right attitude is essential if you are saddled with debt and looking for a way to free yourself. The amount of debt you have will determine how long and detailed your plan must be. The larger the debt, the longer it will take to eliminate it, and the more dedicated and determined you must become. Make no mistake, without a plan, the debt hangs around.

Knocking out the debt is only the first part of the puzzle. The second part of the puzzle is calming the lifestyle responsible for giving birth to the debt. Once the debt has been conquered, it is time to conquer the lifestyle and the spending, in order to stay out of debt. Unless you uncover the root of the problem, your fix is only temporary; you have not permanently solved anything.

So, when tackling debt, you settle the problem first, which is the debt itself. Then you take steps to resolve the cause of the problem, which is the lifestyle, so that the hard work to clear up the debt is not done in vain and you don't land back into a similar situation. Paying off debt is a battle that takes an incredible amount of focus and dedication.

The real work never really ends when it comes to keeping the lifestyle tamed. It becomes a lifelong journey to remain free of debt. Just as recovered drug addicts must take precautions not to re-engage in any activity that could open the door to more drugs; you must take precautions to stay away from the things that landed you in debt. Friends and relatives often pay a big part in your success to become debt free and can also play a part is landing you be back where you came from, in debt again.

Believe it or not, regardless of your age, peer pressure plays a big part as to whether you will succeed in your plan to become debt free. Your friends and co-workers typically have a tremendous influence over how, when, and what you spend your money on. Peer pressure has as much to do with getting into debt as it does with getting out of debt. We make purchases, not only to satisfy our own needs, but to impress others to gain approval or to simply keep up in the "possessions" race with our friends, co-workers, and neighbors. Those of you who think peer pressure if just for teens, think again. Peer pressure is still prevalent in both single adults and married couples. The pressure is applied in the same manner as it is applied on teenagers only with an adult twist to it. When teens seek approval, they go along with and do what the crowd wants to do, regardless of how they personally feel about a situation. This is done strictly to gain acceptance. As adults, we seek the same acceptance. We do this by making purchases to impress our circle of friends. The higher the perceived class of friends, the more money it takes to impress. Whether you are a teen or an adult, you need to be responsible enough not to get caught up in the pressure of believing that you need to do or have certain things in your life just to be accepted.

Take for instance a single person who is on a payment plan to become debt free. After a couple of months on the plan, it becomes increasingly harder to stay focused without a support system in place. This person will be more prone to straying from the payment plan.

After a long exhaustive week at work, it will not be that difficult to be persuaded by co-workers to head out after work on a Friday to blow off some steam. Before you know it, that person is throwing down the credit card and now has new charges. An unplanned expense has just occurred. This is money that should have been used to combat the existing debt. In this set of circumstances, there were no safeguards or support in place to prevent this from happening. An invitation and an opportunity to hang out with co-workers took precedent over keeping on track to become debt free. Peer pressure likely played a big role in racking up the new debt.

Married couples are just as prone to peer pressure as any other group, even though marriages come with a built-in support system. Take Arnold and Cindy for example, who are on a focused payment plan to knock out debt. Arnold has been nagged all week to go on a weekend fishing trip with his co-workers. This couple had recently devised a payment plan to get out of debt. Now, he must deal with peer pressure from the office to take the fishing trip, which will certainly detract from the family's debt repayment plan. His payment plan has reached a fork in the road and he is about to detour from his plan to accommodate his co-workers. He would rather have an upset wife than upset co-workers. His payment plan to rid the debt must now take a break, while he diverts that money and points it towards the weekend fishing trip. The fishing trip will cause him to lose focus and the debt will linger around longer because he was simply too weak to say no.
After the weekend fishing trip, he now has $250 of new debt; not to mention an angry wife. Hopefully, he at least comes out of this deal with a lot of fish and able to get back on track.

When a couple commits to coming up with a plan to become debt free, they automatically have a built-in support system to aid and encourage each other to stick with the plan, unlike a single person. Marriages come with built in cheering sections to keep each other on track. In this case that support system failed to do its job. It is like that one piece of steel falling the wrong way during an implosion; it jeopardizes the whole plan.

Once you become committed and have settled on a plan to get yourself out of debt, beware of detours all around you. They come in many different disguises and are designed to disrupt your plan. Regardless of how well your plan is designed to work, you will encounter detours and roadblocks. If you do become sidetracked, it is never too late to restart. It may feel at times that the minute you decide to change your life and become debt free, all your friends come out of the woodwork and try to distract and derail you from accomplishing your goals.

Some distractions you encounter will be unintentional. Part of devising a solid plan is swallowing your pride and being honest with your friends and co-workers about what you are trying to accomplish. Your friends and co-workers will have to understand that you are changing your lifestyle and spending habits and that you will not be able to go and do everything that they want you to do. This is where the sacrificing and the declining of invitations enter the picture. Going and doing everything with your friends is probably what helped get you into debt, in the first place. You are simply reversing course; to get your financial life back on track.

36. Financial House Cleaning - A Birds Eye View of Your Debt

When corporations bring in new leadership to produce greater profits, the first order of business is usually to cut and slash expenses; to make the company financially leaner. With all options on the table, no job or position is safe with a newly hired CEO now at the reins. The new chief has been hired to produce results and the best way to make an immediate impact is by cutting expenses which automatically increases profits. The new CEO is not concerned about whose toes are stepped on or whose feelings are hurt by the changes that are initiated.

In the National Football League, teams go through similar steps corporations go through, to become more profitable and financially fit. In the preseason, teams bring in around 80 players who will try to improve the team for the upcoming season. They will be put through drills and physical tests as their talents are evaluated for the coaches to build the best team possible. The goal is to put the best possible product on the field, by the time the regular season begins. In a matter of a few weeks, the coaches will make waves of cuts to get down to a league required number of players. These will be the best overall players out of the original 80 players. The coaches must assemble the best players that will give their team the greatest chance of winning and ultimately preserve their coaching jobs.

The hardest part of the preseason is making the necessary, painful cuts. These cuts are the start of the delicate process to ultimately produce more wins. More wins translate into more fans purchasing tickets and team merchandise sold.

The goal of any football team or any sporting team for that matter is to sell as many seats and merchandise as possible. The only way to sell seats and team merchandise is by winning games.
No one wants to buy shirts and hats with a losing team's logo plastered across the front of it. The more games you win, the more publicity you get, the more excited the fans get, which translates into more team paraphernalia sold. Winning is good medicine for everyone involved from the owners to the fans. It keeps the coaches, fans, and the owner happy.

Individuals should take the same approach as NFL teams and corporations, when creating budgets for their own households. You, as the household CEO should consider cutting and slashing all bills that are not pertinent to keeping the house running in order for the household to win and become financially fit. Just as a corporate CEO is not concerned about whose toes get stepped on when deciding who stays and who goes. You should take the same approach when finalizing a family budget.

In order to overcome debt, you must devise a well thought out plan of attack. Planning starts with getting organized. Organization is the key to achieving any worthwhile goal. In business, board rooms serve corporations, in providing a private place to game plan and make major decisions, in order to achieve specific company goals. Your kitchen can become your personal board room, when getting organized to eliminate debt and your kitchen table transformed into your battle ground.
This will be where a plan of attack will be drawn up; where you will strategize and look for ways to attack your debt. The kitchen table is where you will get a bird's eye view of your enemy and know exactly what you're up against. By

getting a good look at your enemy, you will know what will be needed to achieve victory. With your kitchen table being converted to your battleground, you will have to search for a new place in your home to eat meals. A battleground is not a pleasant place to have dinner; it could get quite messy.

The first step in devising a proper plan to defeat your debt will be to gather all your monthly and quarterly bills. Once located, spread them out on the kitchen table. Space them out so that you can get a clear and unobstructed view of the enemy –your debt. Take an accurate inventory of all your bills. From this point, hold every dollar accountable and know exactly how much money is leaving your account each month.

You should now be able to see clearly what you have been going to work for and where your money has been going. With everything in plain sight, you now have a different view of your bills and a sudden a sickening feeling fills your entire body. You cannot believe that you actually support and allow some of these bills to hang around. You get angry and vow to eliminate some of these useless and non-essential bills that have been clogging up your life and stealing your dollars.

Once the initial shock and anger subsides, you're ready to put a stop to this nonsense. It's now time to take these new convictions to the next level. You're now ready to put your plan into motion by dividing your table in half. On one side, put the haves, on the other side, put the have nots.
On the "haves" side, put all the bills that are vital to keeping the house operating. These are the essential bills that absolutely must be paid every month. Examples of the "haves" are the electric bill, mortgage, water, and gas bill. On the "have-nots" side of the table, put every other bill left

over. These bills are the ones that can provide you with some wiggle room in your budget and can be eliminated. Examples of these are cable television, newspaper, magazine subscriptions, satellite radio, app subscriptions and gym memberships. When it comes to these items, this is where you must be realistic and willing to make sacrifices. You know that you can live without these "luxuries", but just have never had to do so.

Now you have had a chance to look over all your bills and have some circled and targeted for destruction, but you're still not 100% certain you can totally remove them from your life. You're dying to set these bills free, but you're just not fully convinced you can do it. You're still hesitant and need a little push. Go ahead, hold your breath, and pull the trigger to make your first round of cuts. Even if you start by just eliminating one or two bills, you will prove to yourself that you can do it.

By successfully making it through the crucial first round of cuts, you're now in unchartered territory, for the first time in your life. With some bold moves, you now might be the only person in your office that doesn't have cable television! You never actually thought that you would be able to get this far, but now you have, by pushing forward through the often difficult first round of cuts.

For most people, this is the first glimpse seeing their lives being regained from debt. The power felt by just making the decision to cut a couple of useless bills is exhilarating. What an incredible feeling of accomplishment as you begin to liberate yourself from debt and to taste a tiny bit of freedom. For the first time, you can almost feel the shackles starting to loosen, by taking the initial steps to reclaim freedom.

When you do something for the first time, it is uncomfortable and you're often filled with anxiety, because you're not sure what to expect. It's the same feeling a child gets on the first day when attending a new school. Once you get comfortable living a life without certain bills each month, you're not going to want to return to it. It's like cutting out sugar from your coffee. The toughest period is the first 30 days but then your body gets used to not having sugar. We tend to establish a bond and get attached to these luxuries and have a hard time saying goodbye. We tend to convince ourselves that these useless expenses somehow keep our lives from falling apart. We must think outside the box when it comes to bills.

In order to fully convince yourself that these initial cuts can work, you must go through a full thirty-day cycle. After thirty days, you will see that these bills were not as crucial as you thought and that you will do simply fine without them in your life. You fretted about cutting out your favorite sandwich shop and you found that bringing your lunch to work was not so bad after all. You somehow managed to get by without that expensive cup of coffee and found that the thermos works fine when transporting home-made coffee to the office. The best thing of all; you're still in one piece!

It's time to get excited and fired up about the cuts you have made for the month. Viewing the money, you saved on paper is one of the most rewarding things you will ever experience.

Let's say that in the initial round of cuts, you managed to eliminate $250 from your month. By saving $250 a month, you have just given yourself a $3000 yearly raise. Now, that's something to really get excited about! Job well done! Give yourself a pat on the back.

You will be amazed at how the little cuts can add up to big savings.

Having accomplished this milestone, you're feeling surprisingly good about yourself and have gained confidence with the results you have produced. You now have a spring in your step. With the momentum you have built up it is time to get back to your kitchen table to look for more bills to cut.

Target all of the unnecessary luxuries still remaining after the first round of cuts. These will be the expenses that you gave some thought to in the first round but let them hang around and live for another month.

With all the bills still left on the table, ask yourself this question. Did my parents manage without these expenses? Can I somehow manage?
Cut back to just the bare necessities that you absolutely need to keep the home operating. Remember, if you're going to deliver a massive blow to defeat your debt, you need to rise and go above and beyond. Go ahead and give yourself another raise. The sacrifices you make now will enhance your life down the road.

When I personally make cuts and sacrifices, I like to look at the yearly savings rather than the monthly savings. By looking at it from a yearly perspective, it puts that savings into a much brighter light. You will also be more motivated to make that bill disappear if you look at it from a yearly perspective.

It is more attractive to look at a yearly savings of $240 than to look at shaving off a measly $20 monthly expense. It's just human nature to get more excited over three-digit savings than two-digit savings.

You should continue to always look for ways to cut and improve your bottom line. Examine every current expense and look for ways to cut or save on that expense. It is a full-time job to try and keep as much of your income as you can and not spend it on useless expenses. You constantly must look for ways to save money, especially since inflation doesn't sit still. Earning your money is the easy part of the equation. Keeping it from being spent unwisely is the hard part.

You can easily simplify your life by just taking an accurate inventory of all your monthly bills and cutting the unnecessary expenses out of your life. It is amazing how we allow foolish expenses to come into our lives. Once these expenses are in our lives, we then agree to support them, even if it means showing up for work when we're sick just to have the money to keep them around. It's time to stop being hospitable and start kicking those useless expenses out of your house.

37. Staying out of Debt

If you have crossed the finish line or still working to get there. At times, you probably even questioned whether you really had what it would take to become completely free from debt. "Debt free" really sounds nice, but is it possible? Does it really exist?

Regardless of how long it took to become debt free, you could not help dreaming of what it would feel like once you finally achieved your goal. The dreaming is what kept you focused and hungry to finish the race.
You struggled and sacrificed during your journey. You endured plenty of tests in the form of emergencies and unexpected expenses. You turned down invitations and stayed away from amazon which threatened to derail you from reaching your goal. You might have quit and had to start over again.

Becoming debt free can be the nucleus for even greater works to come now that you have uncovered some hidden confidence. When you have been beat up for a long period of time, you tend to lose all hope and question whether you have enough "will power" to accomplish anything meaningful in life.

By personally battling through a journey to defeat debt, you say to yourself never again will you engage in the careless spending which landed you in debt in the first place. You are adamant that you will never again experience anything like what you have just been through. You are determined that your sacrifices will not be in vain and the lessons learned will not be forgotten. This is easy to say when the fire is still burning inside and the memories of your journey to become debt free are still fresh in your mind.

But how will you feel after you are free of debt and your emotions have subsided a year or two down the road? Will you be able to maintain those same emotions and feelings that you had during your journey to become debt free? How will you then feel about charging an item or financing something that catches your eye? What if you are feeling down and depressed? Are you likely to fall back into debt to fill a temporary void? Will you abandon all your new-found wisdom if these events unfold?

As convicted felons get released from prison, they are full of excitement and vow never to return to their cell. It is a constant battle every day for felons to walk the straight line, especially if a life of crime is all they know. To remain free, they must avoid the temptations that landed them in prison. This can be achieved only if they are deeply committed to changing their lives and are willing to do the things that will keep them from returning to a life of crime. It will take hard work and effort to stay committed to walking the straight line. Having been locked up should serve as a strong deterrent from returning to prison.

It is crucial to always remember the agony you felt while you were shackled by debt. These battle scars should always remain fresh in your mind and serve as a constant reminder of the dangers that come with accumulating debt. Once you have become free of debt, the fight to remain debt free is never completely over. As any recovering alcoholic will tell you, the battle is never over. Getting out of debt is only half the battle; staying there is the other half. To remain out of debt, you must continue to always remain true to the beliefs and principles that convinced you and guided you out of debt in the first place.

Having gone through this life changing journey of becoming debt free, you emerged a little bruised and battered but a much smarter and confident person. What did not kill you along the journey, made your views and attitude toward debt that much stronger. God bless you and Good luck to you.

The End

www.ingramcontent.com/pod-product-compliance
Lightning Source LLC
LaVergne TN
LVHW091146080826
845145LV00008B/2277